EL SALVADOR
in Pictures

Francesca Davis DiPiazza

TF
CB

Twenty-First Century Books

Contents

Website address: www.lernerbooks.com

Twenty-First Century Books
A division of Lerner Publishing Group, Inc.
241 First Avenue North
Minneapolis, MN 55401 U.S.A.

Library of Congress Cataloging-in-Publication Data

DiPiazza, Francesca, 1961–
   El Salvador in pictures / by Francesca Davis DiPiazza—Rev. & expanded.
      p.   cm. — (Visual geography series)
   Includes bibliographical references and index.
   ISBN: 978-0-8225-7145-2 (lib. bdg. : alk. paper)
   1. El Salvador—Juvenile literature. 2. El Salvador—Pictorial works. I. Title.
F1483.2.D57 2008
972.8405022'2—dc22   2006035006

Manufactured in the United States of America
2 3 4 5 6 7 - BP - 13 12 11 10 09 08

INTRODUCTION

A popular saying in El Salvador advises, in Spanish, *El que quiera celeste, que le cueste,* meaning, "Whoever wants blue sky has to work for it." The people of this Spanish-speaking country have had to work hard in the face of many challenges. These include a bloody civil war from 1980 to 1992, a wide gap between rich and poor people, and frequent natural disasters.

The Central American nation of El Salvador is one of the smallest nations in the Western Hemisphere. With a population of 7 million, it is also one of the most crowded. The land fronts the Pacific Ocean on the south and is backed by a volcanic mountain chain. Volcanic eruptions, earthquakes, and hurricanes continually threaten the country. Farms cover much of the land, and little of the original rain forest remains.

People have lived in the area of El Salvador for thousands of years. The Pipil people were the largest native group when Spanish conquerors arrived in 1524. The Pipiles called their fertile land Cuscatlán, which means "Land of Riches."

The struggle for limited land has dominated the country's history. During the Spanish colonial era, Spanish settlers took over the land and suppressed or enslaved the native people. A few rich landowners controlled most of the country. Most people worked for little pay on large farms or struggled to survive on tiny plots of land. Independence from Spain in 1821 did little to change the situation.

The late 1800s saw the development of coffee-growing in the rich volcanic soil of the highlands. When world coffee prices collapsed after 1929, farmworkers organized unions. They sought reforms in landownership and working conditions. In 1932 farmworkers in the west staged an uprising. In response, government forces massacred thousands of the area's inhabitants to crush all opposition. Afterward, the army enforced the division between the wealthy landowners and the poor and unschooled peasants.

The unequal distribution of land and wealth eventually brought violence to the country again. In 1980 civil war broke out between

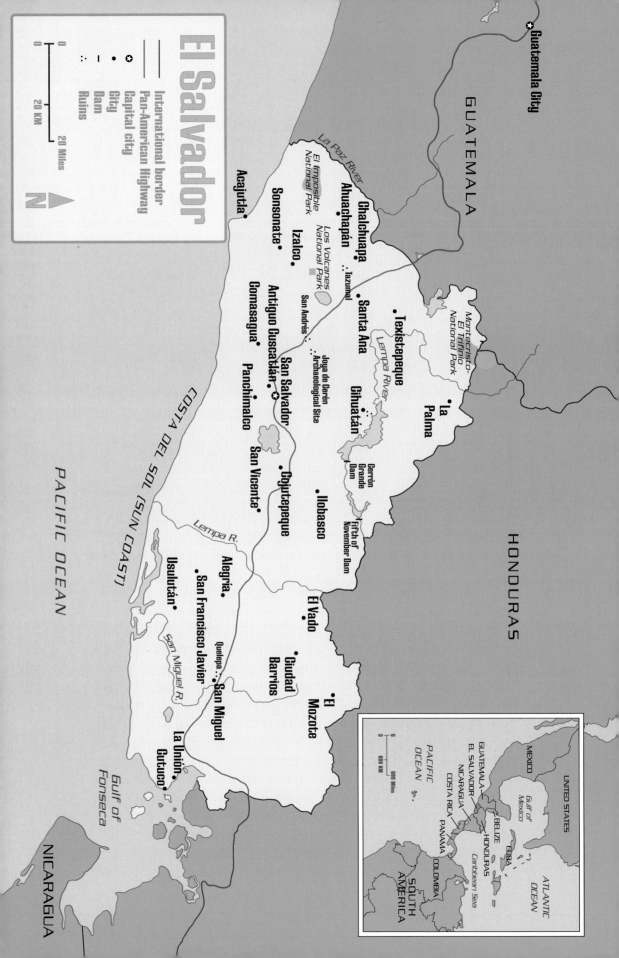

El Salvador

Legend:
- International border
- Pan-American Highway
- Capital City
- City
- Dam
- Ruins

N

0 20 KM
0 20 Miles

GUATEMALA

✪ Guatemala City

HONDURAS

NICARAGUA

PACIFIC OCEAN

Gulf of Fonseca

La Paz River

Acajutla

Sonsonate

Ahuachapán

Chalchuapa

Izalco

El Imposible National Park

Los Volcanes National Park

Tazumal

San Andrés

Santa Ana

Comasagua

Antiguo Cuscatlán

San Salvador ✪

Panchimalco

San Vicente

Cojutepeque

Joya de Cerén Archaeological Site

Texistepeque

Cihuatán

Lempa River

Montecristo-El Trifinio National Park

la Palma

Cerrón Grande Dam

Fifth of November Dam

Ilobasco

Lempa R.

San Miguel R.

COSTA DEL SOL (SUN COAST)

Usulután

Alegria

San Francisco Javier

Quelepa

San Miguel

El Vado

Ciudad Barrios

El Mozote

La Unión

Conchagua

UNITED STATES

MEXICO

Gulf of Mexico

BELIZE

GUATEMALA

EL SALVADOR

HONDURAS

NICARAGUA

COSTA RICA

PANAMA

CUBA

Caribbean Sea

COLOMBIA

SOUTH AMERICA

ATLANTIC OCEAN

PACIFIC OCEAN

N

0 800 KM
0 800 Miles

government forces and rebels of the Farabundo Martí National Liberation Front (FMLN is the recognized Spanish-language acronym). The FMLN demanded basic changes in landownership. FMLN guerrilla groups—bands of rebels—destroyed roads, factories, and other government targets. In retaliation, the military government imposed a state of siege on the country. Government death squads committed atrocities against anyone they suspected of supporting the FMLN. Financial and military aid to both sides by foreign countries—including the United States—prolonged and worsened the conflict. The hardworking Salvadorans suffered as their economy collapsed. Two million refugees fled the country.

Because of El Salvador's thumb-like shape, Salvadorans nicknamed their country El Pulgarcito—Spanish for "little thumb."

Years of attacks and counterattacks exhausted both sides. With no one winning, the government and the rebel forces signed a peace agreement in 1992. The conflict had killed more than 75,000 people and left the economy in ruins. A long list of reforms transformed the country. New laws allowed the FMLN to take part in elections. Land-reform laws gave some land to poor farming families. The government improved health care and education. Foreign companies and Salvadorans again invested money in the country.

Even at peace, El Salvador faced many challenges. After the war, the country's crime rate soared, and it remains high. A series of natural disasters hit the country. The most damaging of these were Hurricane Mitch in 1998 and two earthquakes in 2001. The nation was left struggling to get back on its feet.

Despite troubles, democracy has taken firm hold in El Salvador. A high percentage of Salvadorans voted in the 2004 presidential election. They elected Elías Antonio "Tony" Saca. He promised to put the divisions of the past behind. In 2006 the Central America Free Trade Agreement (CAFTA) between El Salvador and the United States went into effect. This agreement improves trade between the two countries. Salvadorans hope that with continued peace and hard work they will see more blue sky in the future.

THE LAND

The Republic of El Salvador covers an area of 8,124 square miles (21,041 square kilometers). Almost as big as Massachusetts, it is the smallest country in Central America. El Salvador measures about 150 miles (241 km) from west to east. The country stretches 50 miles (80 km) from north to south.

Much of El Salvador is mountainous, like its neighbors. Guatemala is El Salvador's neighbor to the west. Honduras borders it on the north and east. The Gulf of Fonseca also forms a portion of El Salvador's eastern boundary. Nicaragua lies across the gulf, to the east. El Salvador shares the gulf's waters with Honduras and Nicaragua. It also owns several small islands in the gulf. The Pacific Ocean forms El Salvador's southern border.

Topography

El Salvador has three main regions, each running from east to west. Altitude, or height above sea level, determines each region. Salvadorans

call the Coastal Lowlands region the *tierra caliente,* which means "hot land" in Spanish, the nation's official language. The lowlands run the length of the Pacific coast and extend 10 to 20 miles (16 to 32 km) inland. The region consists of wetlands and a flat, fertile plain. Large commercial farms called haciendas cover much of the plain. Farmers there raise cotton and sugarcane or graze cattle. The black-sand beaches along the coast are of volcanic origin. Imposing cliffs rise out of the ocean. They separate the beaches from one another.

The Central Highlands exist at an average altitude of 2,000 feet (610 meters). The region supports most of the country's farms, industries, and people. The highlands' central plateau is a broad valley between two mountain ranges—the southern coastal range and the northern interior highlands. The higher slopes in the central highlands are ideal for growing coffee. The land on the lower slopes is farmed intensively to feed a rapidly growing population. Salvadorans call the Central Highlands the *tierra templada* (land of moderate climate).

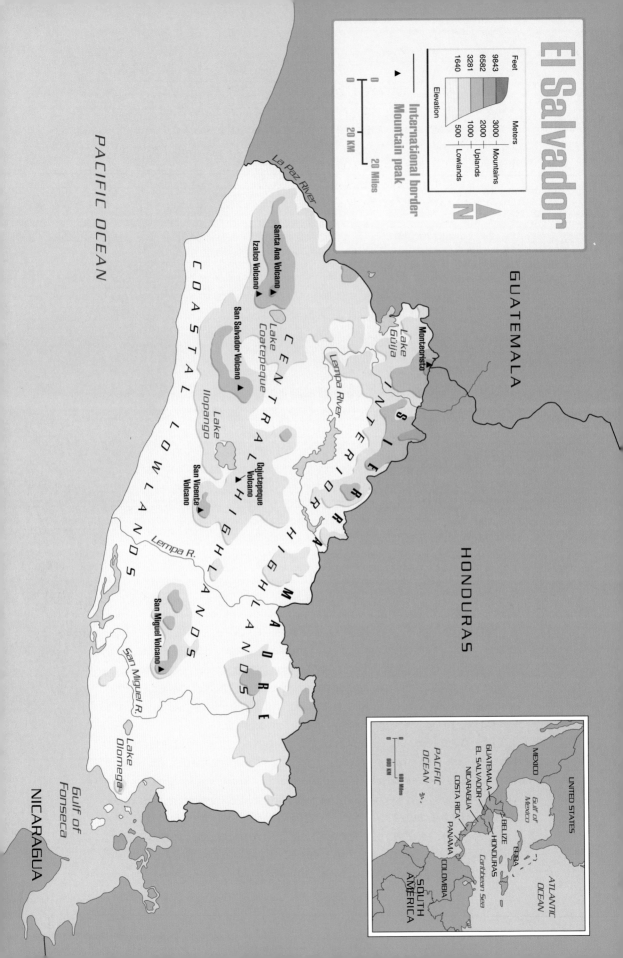

El Salvador

N

Elevation

▲ Mountain peak

—— International border

Feet	Meters	
9843	3000	Mountains
6582	2000	Uplands
3281	1000	
1640	500	Lowlands

0
20 KM

0
20 Miles

GUATEMALA

HONDURAS

PACIFIC OCEAN

NICARAGUA

Gulf of
Fonseca

La Paz River

Lake
Güija

Montecristo

Santa Ana Volcano

Izalco Volcano ▲

San Salvador Volcano ▲

Lake
Coatepeque

Lake
Ilopango

C E N T R A L

Lempa River

I N T E R I O R

S I E R R A

San Vicente
Volcano ▲

Cojutepeque
Volcano ▲

H I G H L A N D S

C O A S T A L   L O W L A N D S

Lempa R.

M A D R E

San Miguel Volcano ▲

San Miguel R.

Lake
Olomega

UNITED STATES

MEXICO

Gulf of
Mexico

CUBA

ATLANTIC
OCEAN

BELIZE

GUATEMALA
EL SALVADOR
NICARAGUA
COSTA RICA

HONDURAS

Caribbean Sea

PANAMA

COLOMBIA

SOUTH
AMERICA

PACIFIC
OCEAN

0   600 Miles

0   600 KM

The northern Interior Highlands also enjoy a temperate climate. Salvadorans call the region *tierra fria* (cold land) because the high altitude keeps the temperatures lower. But the harsh landscape is unwelcoming, and few people live in the region. The Sierra Madre mountain range creates a rugged, rocky region. The Lempa River forms valleys in the highlands. Wherever it is possible to cultivate the soil, a farm or small settlement is tucked into the mountainous terrain.

◐ Volcanoes

Known as the Land of Volcanoes, El Salvador has more than twenty volcanoes. Volcanoes are openings in the earth's surface where heat and lava (molten rock) escape from below. Despite the danger, cities developed near volcanoes because ash and sediment from their eruptions create fertile soil. Travelers sometimes cross large expanses of jagged, black basalt—the residue of past eruptions—on Salvadoran roads. Most of El Salvador's volcanoes are dormant (inactive). Clear, blue lakes fill the craters of many long-dormant volcanoes. Montecristo is the country's highest point, at 7,933 feet (2,418 m) above sea level.

Six active volcanoes sit in the Central Highlands. They rise at regular intervals from west to east, adding a dramatic accent to the landscape. Santa Ana Volcano (also called Ilamatepec) rises to 7,800 feet (2,377 m). It overlooks the city of Santa Ana. Volcanoes also overlook San Salvador (the capital), Cojutepeque, San Vicente, and San Miguel. Izalco Volcano is located near the Pacific Ocean. It erupted continuously for nearly two centuries until 1966. Sailors called it the Lighthouse of the Pacific and used its fire as a beacon. Scientists consider Izalco to be "at rest," or not completely dormant. Volcanic activity remains a constant threat in El Salvador. The Santa Ana Volcano erupted in 2005 after being dormant since 1904.

Heat from the earth's interior is also evident in geysers, which shoot up hot water and steam. A power plant in the west traps geothermal (earth) heat to create electrical power.

> The horseshoe-shaped Pacific Ocean rim is commonly called the Ring of Fire because of its high number of volcanoes. In El Salvador, people call it Cinturon del Fuego, Spanish for "Belt of Fire." Volcanic activity and earthquakes are common all around the edge of the Pacific Ocean. Shifts in the tectonic plates that form the earth's surface cause these violent land movements.

Many earthquakes also occur in El Salvador. The devastating 1986 earthquake in San Salvador registered 7.5 on the Richter scale.

Rivers and Lakes

Hundreds of rivers, streams, and creeks crisscross El Salvador. The Lempa River is the only major river on which boats can travel. The river rises in Guatemala. Its waters are brown with silt, or bits of soil, from the mountains they through which they pass. The Lempa forms part of the border with Honduras before it empties into the Pacific. Farmers cultivate the fertile lands along the Lempa, down to the river's edge. Some 150 smaller rivers feed into the river. These waterways drain a large area of El Salvador. Dams on the Lempa—such as the Fifth of November and Cerrón Grande dams—harness the power of the river's flow. The dams' hydroelectric plants provide 35 percent of El Salvador's electricity. Two less important rivers—the La Paz River on the Guatemalan border and the San Miguel River in eastern El Salvador—drain smaller areas.

The country's four major lakes all formed in extinct volcanoes. These crater lakes are called calderas. They provide popular places to swim and fish. Lake Güija is on the Guatemalan border in the northwest. Lake Olomega is in the east. Lake Coatepeque is west and Lake Ilopango is east of San Salvador. Many small lakes also dot the countryside.

Lake Coatepeque (*above*) fills a volcanic crater. Next to it, smoke rises from Santa Ana Volcano.

Climate

El Salvador is located in the tropics—the region of the earth near the equator. The climate in the tropics does not vary much during the year. But El Salvador's many altitudes do vary its climate. Most Salvadorans live in the Central Highlands. There the average temperature is a pleasant 73°F (23°C) year-round. In contrast, along the Pacific coast it is often oppressively hot and humid. Temperatures there average 83°F (28°C).

The country experiences distinct wet and dry seasons. The rainy season extends from May to October. During this season, rain showers fall almost every afternoon. During the dry season the rest of the year, light rains occur. Annual rainfall amounts to 60 inches (152 centimeters) in the central and interior highlands. Along the coast, average rainfall increases to 85 inches (216 cm).

Flora and Fauna

Dense tropical rain forests once covered much of El Salvador. In modern times, only 3 percent of these original forests exist. Despite heavy land use, more kinds of trees grow in El Salvador than in Europe. The forests mainly survive in mountainous areas with few people. The trees here are deciduous (leaf-shedding). Some common trees are dogwood, mahogany, walnut, rubber, and ceiba.

In less rugged areas, grasslands and sparse forests of oak, cedar, and pine are found. Many medicinal plants grow in lowland areas. Coconut, mango, and other tropical fruit trees are also numerous. Mangrove swamps fringe estuaries (where rivers meet the sea). Mangrove trees can survive in salty water. Their roots grow partly aboveground.

Many flowers grow in El Salvador, and the nation exports cut flowers. The *izote* is El Salvador's national flower. Two hundred kinds of orchids bloom in El Salvador. These epiphytes, or air plants, grow on trees and take their moisture from the humid air.

El Salvador is home to more than four hundred kinds of birds, including parrots, toucans, hummingbirds, and vultures. The southern plain is home to the quetzal, a beautiful, bright-plumed bird. The quetzal was a sacred bird to the ancient Mayan people of Central America. Throughout the country, five hundred kinds of butterflies also add color to the air.

Reptiles are also common. The land's many kinds of lizards include iguanas, and its many kinds of snakes include rattlesnakes and boa constrictors. Crocodiles, caimans, and alligators live in the lagoons of the south.

Offshore, the Pacific waters abound with fish, including groupers, mullet, anchovies, tuna, and sea bass. Shrimp is a major export item. Marine animals include sharks and sea turtles.

Deer, pumas, coyotes, armadillos, and peccaries—a kind of wild pig—survive in the mountains. Tapirs also live in the mountains. Their black and white coloring provides camouflage in shadowy forests. Visitors to the rain forests would be lucky to spot one of the rare jaguars, ocelots, margays, or other kinds of endangered big cats. Squirrels, rabbits, and weasels are common in El Salvador.

Natural Resources and Environmental Issues

El Salvador is poor in mineral resources. Small amounts of gold and silver exist in the mountains of the northeast. El Salvador has large quantities of quartz, gypsum, limestone, and pumice.

The country's hardwood trees—including mahogany and walnut—support a furniture industry. The balsa tree's light and buoyant wood has long been used for boat building. Another valuable tree is the balsam, El Salvador's national tree. It produces a sticky reddish-brown substance used in perfumes, candies, and medicines.

El Salvador faces serious environmental challenges. Deforestation, or the loss of woodlands, is one of the most pressing concerns. The country's rate of deforestation is the highest in Central America. It loses 3 percent of its forests every year. People remove trees to make farmland or pasture for cattle. Villagers rely on wood for cooking and heating fuel. Tree roots hold soil in place, and their loss leads to soil erosion. Rain washes away fertile layers of dirt, leaving the land barren.

El Salvador also suffers from pollution. Industrial wastes and raw sewage contaminate soil and water. Some foreign companies ship toxic waste to El Salvador to store.

The name of El Salvador's national park El Imposible is Spanish for "the impossible." In the early 1900s, coffee growers shipped their harvest through the area's mountains on mules. The trip included crossing a steep river gorge called the Impossible Pass. Wobbly bridges crossed the gorge. Sometimes they broke, and travelers fell to their deaths.

Pollution and the densely settled human population have led to the loss of El Salvador's once-abundant wildlife. Sixty-eight kinds of birds and eighteen kinds of mammals are already extinct. Ninety more wildlife species are endangered, or threatened with dying out.

El Salvador's people and government are beginning to take steps to protect their natural heritage. In schools around the country, children celebrate Earth Day every year. Several national parks exist, and more protected areas are being established. El

Most big cats kill their prey by biting the throat, but a **jaguar** uses its powerful jaws to crush the back of its prey's skull. To learn more about El Salvador's endangered wildlife, go to www.vgsbooks.com for links.

Imposible National Park is the largest of the parks. It is one of the last remains of original rain forest in Central America.

Besides human-made challenges, El Salvador also faces severe natural hazards. Earthquakes, volcanoes, and hurricanes frequently damage the country. Human factors increase some of these dangers. Chemicals from industry have increased global warming, or the gradual rise in the earth's temperature. The surface temperature of the ocean has risen too. The warmer water causes hurricanes to increase in force. Furthermore, warmer water expands, causing sea levels to rise. This affects low-lying areas of El Salvador's coastline. Human factors also add to earthquakes' destructive powers. People cut down trees, whose roots anchor the land. Earthquakes then cause massive landslides on the treeless ground.

"GREEN" COFFEE

Coffee plantations cover 9 percent of El Salvador's land. Some farmers use "green," or ecologically friendly, ways to cultivate coffee. They plant trees to shade their coffee bushes. The trees provide shelter for birds and other animals. Coffee plantations link two national parks: El Imposible and Los Volcanes. The plantations' trees create a pathway for wildlife to travel the 31 miles (50 km) between the natural forests. This pathway gives the area's animals a better chance for survival. On one of the plantations, observers recorded 120 species of birds.

Cities

The native people of El Salvador first established cities thousands of years ago. Archaeologists, or scientists who study the remains of early cultures, continue to explore these ancient cities. Spanish conquerors and settlers after 1525 built cities in Spanish style, often on the sites of ancient cities. During the civil war of the 1980s, peasants fled to cities to escape rural violence. The cities did not have enough jobs and housing for all the newcomers. Their presence swelled the size of slums in the capital and in cities near the worst fighting. Though El Salvador's modern big cities offer fast food restaurants and shopping malls, their slums remain places of extreme poverty. Unemployment and crime are high, and hunger is common.

SAN SALVADOR (population 1.5 million) is the capital and largest city of El Salvador. It is the country's commercial, cultural, and political center. Located at an elevation of about 2,000 feet (610 m), San Salvador enjoys a mild climate. Days are often hot, and nights are pleasant.

San Salvador Volcano makes a beautiful but dangerous backdrop for **San Salvador,** El Salvador's capital city.

The indigenous (native) Pipil people established the first city in the area of present-day San Salvador in 1054. In 1525 Spanish troops invaded the area and established their capital. These Christian forces named the new city San Salvador, which means "Holy Savior." An earthquake in 1854 destroyed San Salvador. The rebuilt, modern city is 25 miles (40 km) south of its original site. Few architectural reminders of its Spanish past remain.

San Salvador is Central America's most crowded city. The noise, grime, and press of people can be overwhelming. Vehicle fumes add to the city's low-hanging smog. Rush hour creates a bedlam of bumper-to-bumper traffic. The hills around the city trap the air pollution.

During the long midday siesta (lunch break), the heart of the city undergoes a welcome change. There is leisure time to admire the ornate National Palace, where the legislature (lawmaking body) meets, and to visit excellent museums. The unique Iglesia el Rosario (Rosary Church) features a soaring arched roof. Statues made of scrap metal adorn the interior. After dark, however, crime makes the city's downtown streets dangerous.

Beyond the downtown area lie attractive suburbs. Set at a higher altitude, the city's suburbs have broad, tree-lined streets. San Salvador's middle and upper classes live in ranch-style homes with fine lawns and gardens.

SANTA ANA (population 254,000) is El Salvador's second-largest city. Unemployment and slums afflict Santa Ana, like the capital. However, wide, clean streets and old buildings in good condition make

Coffee export taxes paid for construction of the Santa Ana Theater in Santa Ana. Construction began in 1902.

the city much more pleasant. Located in the west, the area has been inhabited since about the A.D. 500s. Coffee and sugarcane plantations are the main industries supporting the modern city.

Santa Ana's original name in the native language Nahuatl was Cihuatehuacan. The name means "Place of Holy Women." Early Native American residents believed that *tehuas* (priestesses or holy women) could communicate with spirits and affect nature.

SAN MIGUEL (population 245,000) is the main hub city in the east. The active San Miguel Volcano looms over the city. It hasn't erupted since 1986. Some of the country's richest coffee lands lie on its slopes. The city is also the country's center for cotton and henequen. Henequen is a fiber used to make rope and hammocks. During the civil war, San Miguel's population swelled with rural dwellers fleeing the fighting. The end of the war in 1992 allowed some of these farmers to return home. But many stayed in search of a new livelihood. Peace brought an economic boom, and the city bustles with trade and markets. The busy city suffers from air pollution.

SONSONATE (popuation 127,000) in western El Salvador is known for its colorful festivities held during the week before Easter. The city's population more than doubled during the war.

ILOBASCO (population 80,000) is a northern mountain village famous for its ceramic artists. The Lenca people were the original inhabitants. Modern artisans produce painted plates, jars, dolls, and other clay objects for sale in the city's shops. Teachers pass on the skill at a local school for ceramic art.

LA UNIÓN (population 64,000) in the southeast is the main port on the Gulf of Fonseca. Its facilities are able to handle large oceangoing vessels. It is also the departure point to reach El Salvador's islands in the gulf.

Visit www.vgsbooks.com for links to websites with additional information about El Salvador's major cities, its rural and wild areas, its volatile land and weather, and its environmental issues.

Workers in Acajutla pack shrimp for export.

ACAJUTLA (population 24,000) in the west is one of Central America's busiest and most modern ports. Much of El Salvador's coffee is exported from here. Tourists pass through, on the way to nearby beaches. Surfing is good on the coast to the east.

HISTORY AND GOVERNMENT

According to archaeologists, people first lived in the area of present-day El Salvador more than five thousand years ago. There are various theories as to why and how they came. The most widely accepted view is that people traveled on a land bridge from Asia to North America about twenty-five thousand years ago. Gradually they migrated throughout the Americas.

Early Civilizations

The Olmecs were the earliest known people in all of Middle America. (Mexico and Central America together are called Middle America.) The center of Olmec culture was near the present-day Mexican city of Veracruz. It reached its height of power about 2000 B.C. Olmecs also migrated to El Salvador. They left carvings of fierce warriors on the Olmec Boulder, found near Chalchuapa.

A people known as the Lencas lived in El Salvador, perhaps as long ago as 300 B.C. The Lencas' main base was at Usulután, in eastern El

Salvador. From there, they traveled widely, trading their distinctive pottery. The Lencas absorbed influences from several other cultures, possibly even from as far away as the Inca culture in South America.

By A.D. 500, Aztecs from Teotihuacán, just north of Mexico City, reached El Salvador. Ruins near the present-day city of Ahuachapán display Aztec design. After the fall of Teotihuacán in about A.D. 650, the destruction of Aztec temples in El Salvador gives evidence that their power came to an abrupt and total end. Their sculptures and monuments were broken, defaced, and buried. After that time, the Toltecs, another people whose culture stemmed from further north of Mexico City, came to El Salvador. But they too eventually faded from the scene.

The Maya were a highly cultured civilization. Their cities stretched from southern Mexico to Honduras. El Salvador became one of the centers of the Mayan civilization. It is uncertain when the Maya became El Salvador's most important inhabitants. However, their language and religion were in use in the area 1,500 years ago. Mayans prayed to the sun and moon. They tried to please other important deities such as the rain god and corn god. Imposing temple ruins and ceremonial plazas are found at Tazumal, Cihuatán, San Andrés, and Quelepa. The Maya built these sites between A.D. 500 and 1000. The ruins testify to the Mayans' skills as architects and engineers. Mayan merchants were important, widely traveled people. In addition to trading goods, the merchants exchanged information and ideas.

The Pipiles

The Pipil people originated in southern Mexico and spoke the Nahuatl language. They reached El Salvador about A.D. 1000, just as the Mayan period was ending. The Pipiles eventually occupied almost all of El Salvador and neighboring areas of modern-day Honduras and Nicaragua. They grew to be the largest of several native groups in El Salvador. For five centuries, they lived a settled, farming existence. Culturally, they were not as advanced as the Maya. They borrowed many Mayan traits. But they were tough, warlike, and usually victorious. They built their capital near San Salvador, close to the present-day town of Cihuatán. Traces of the once-powerful Pipiles are found there and throughout El Salvador.

Like other inhabitants of Central America, the Pipiles grew corn as their main food. They worshipped corn gods and rain gods. They regulated their lives—the times of planting, harvesting, and major ceremonies—using the accurate Mayan or Aztec calendar. The Pipiles were skilled in mathematics, architecture, and astronomy. Pipil craftspeople excelled in weaving, pottery making, stone carving, and the working of gold and silver.

Spanish Rule

The Pipil civilization attracted the interest and greed of Spanish explorers and conquistadores (conquerors). Hernando Cortés was the captain general (royal representative) of New Spain—as Mexico was then called. In 1523 he sent his lieutenant Pedro de Alvarado to conquer Central America. After overrunning Guatemala, in 1524 Alvarado and his troops entered present-day El Salvador. The Pipiles and other indigenous groups put up a good fight. In their first battle, the Pipiles defeated the Spaniards and wounded Alvarado. This was one of the few major defeats of the conquistadores anywhere in the Americas. Although the different native groups greatly outnumbered the Spanish, they did not unite to resist the conquest. The unified Spaniards had superior military

Pedro de Alvarado became the first Spanish governor of El Salvador and Guatemala, serving from from 1524 until his death in 1541.

strength. Therefore, the Spanish defeated the Pipiles and took over their capital within a year.

From 1525 the territory and people of El Salvador were part of Spain's empire in the Western Hemisphere. El Salvador became a province of New Spain. A captain general ruled the region of El Salvador. His headquarters were in Guatemala. The first city called San Salvador was founded in 1525, near the former Pipil capital Cuscatlán. In 1526 an earthquake destroyed the city. In 1545 San Salvador was built in its present location.

Colonial rule would last almost three hundred years. It destroyed the Native Americans' governing systems. Societies weakened as large numbers of indigenous people died from European diseases. The Spanish also destroyed native religions and cultural traditions. Christian missionaries, or religious teachers, converted the indigenous people to the Roman Catholic religion, sometimes by force. They introduced schools to teach Spanish culture and language.

THE DESTRUCTION OF THE INDIANS

Spanish conquerors and missionaries in Central America often treated native people, or Indians, harshly. But one Spanish missionary—Father Bartolomé de las Casas (1484–1566)—spoke out against forced labor and forced religious conversions. He criticized Spanish brutality in his book *A Brief Account of the Destruction of the Indians* (1552). He wrote that Christianity is useless "as long as innumerable human beings are slaughtered in a war waged on the excuse of . . . spreading religion." In response, Spain passed laws protecting Indian rights in Central America. But Spanish settlers largely ignored the laws. Las Casas remains a hero in modern El Salvador.

Under a system called the *encomienda,* the Spanish demanded unpaid work from the native people. The Pipiles built colonial towns and churches, adding their own unmistakable designs to the ornamentation.

Before long, the bloodlines of the conquerors and the conquered were blended. People of mixed Spanish and native heritage are called mestizos. Those who adopted the Spanish way of life were called ladinos. The blending process was not always peaceful. Every so often during the colonial period, the Pipiles rebelled. Each time, the Spanish put them down with bloody reprisals. Violence, disease, and hard, forced labor killed many of the native people.

During centuries of colonial rule, El Salvador was largely undeveloped land between Guatemala and Nicaragua. Few settlers were interested in land where mineral resources were scarce. Furthermore, because so many native people had died, there was little cheap labor available. It was too expensive for most settlers to import African people to work as slaves. Lacking an Atlantic coastline, the country missed out on shipping trade. The Spanish crown paid little attention to the small province that couldn't pay much in taxes. El Salvador was considered sleepy and backward—and one of the least important parts of the vast Spanish Empire. It was largely left alone for 250 years.

The colony became more active in the later 1700s. The production of cattle, cacao, and indigo—a deep-blue dye—became profitable and widespread. Spanish landowners became wealthy raising crops for export. Meanwhile, most people survived by raising corn and beans on small plots of land. The Catholic Church and the military supported the wealthy, elite class that ruled society. The widespread production of cash crops (salable crops) set the pattern for El Salvador's future.

Struggle for Independence

The successful American and French revolutions of the late 1700s inspired Spain's colonies. The revolutionary ideas of liberty and democracy awakened Salvadoran yearnings for freedom from Spain.

The first serious challenge to Spanish rule in Central America took place in El Salvador. French emperor Napoleon Bonaparte invaded Spain in 1808. Salvadorans took advantage of Spain's troubles at this time. In 1811 a local Catholic priest, José Matías Delgado, started a

Investigate the history of Spain's conquest of Central America in the 1500s. Find out about colonial El Salvador and its struggle for independence. Go to www.vgsbooks.com for links.

revolt to gain independence. Spain sternly put down this action. But it led to uprisings in Guatemala and Nicaragua. Three years later, Salvadoran Manuel José Arce led another revolt. Spain suppressed this, too.

Independence finally came to El Salvador as part of an action taken by all the Central American provinces. In 1821 representatives from all the Central American countries met in Guatemala City. There, on September 15, they signed the Declaration of Independence from Spain.

That same year, Mexico won its independence under the leadership of Agustín de Iturbide. He then tried to force El Salvador to join his empire. The threat was short-lived, however. In 1823 Iturbide was killed. El Salvador was free to follow its own destiny.

Spain's other Central American colonies also won their independence during this time. In 1823 El Salvador became part of the United Provinces of Central America. The other members were Honduras, Guatemala, Nicaragua, and Costa Rica. The federation, or union, chose Guatemala City as its capital. Manuel José Arce was its first president. José Matías Delgado supervised the writing of the federation's constitution.

From the outset, strife among different groups threatened this experiment in regional govern-ment. As a rule, liberals favored decentralized, or

Manuel José Arce

local, governments. They also wanted the Catholic Church to have less power and influence. Conservatives, in contrast, looked to the Church as a pillar of support. They backed strong central governments con-trolled by wealthy landowners.

By 1827 the federation was wracked by civil conflict. Armed groups representing various political positions terrorized many parts of the federation. In 1838 Rafael Carrera, a Guatemalan, spearheaded a con-servative-backed revolt. The United Provinces of Central America col-lapsed. El Salvador began its life as an independent republic in 1838, as a result of Carrera's Guatemalan revolution.

◉ Nationhood

For the next two decades, liberal and conservative governments alternated in power in El Salvador. The nation engaged in several short wars with its neighbors, including battles with Honduras in 1845. A long series of short-term presidents followed. Revolutions overthrew five of them. Two were assassinated. El Salvador's violent experience with democratic self-rule was the norm for most other Latin American countries at this time.

Salvadoran soldiers line up for duty in the late 1800s. A population census taken in 1858 had revealed that the national army forced young poor men to become soldiers. The government also required campesinos more than fifteen years old to work for two days every week building roads.

During this era, a small group of landowners and merchants increased El Salvador's production of cash crops. New synthetic dyes in the 1870s ended the demand for indigo. Coffee replaced indigo as the leading export earner. It became so important, Salvadorans called it King Coffee.

Coffee growing was a huge economic success for El Salvador. Coffee grows best in the cool, high hillsides of the nation. The few remaining indigenous people owned this land in common, not individually. In 1882 the government passed a law against communal ownership. This allowed coffee growers to seize the land.

By the late 1800s, about 2 percent of Salvadorans owned 75 percent of the land. The vast majority of Salvadorans were landless peasants or rural laborers called campesinos. Coffee brought in most of the country's money. However, the ruling classes spent little money on social improvements for the nation, especially in the rural areas. For example, they didn't think campesinos needed education. Therefore, rural education was poorly funded.

A few ruling families held political and economic power. Salvadorans called this oligarchy (small ruling group) Los Catorce Grandes, or the Fourteen Families. This elite group used their power to support and further their own interests. Under these conditions, political power changed hands peacefully. In theory, the government followed a constitution and democratic procedures. In reality, the oligarchy appointed governments that would help them keep their privileges.

In the early twentieth century, rural life in El Salvador did not change much. Urban development boomed, however. Workers in cities began to form labor unions to get better working conditions and pay. These organizations attracted the attention of rural coffee workers, too. Soon the government declared labor unions illegal. In 1912 the government founded a rural police force called the National Guard. One of the guard's duties was to keep campesinos from organizing. They arrested and even killed campesinos who tried to start unions during the 1920s.

In 1929 a worldwide economic depression led to falling prices for El Salvador's coffee. Hard times hit the country, which depended on coffee earnings. In the face of widespread discontent, the newly founded Salvadoran Communist Party promoted land reforms to distribute land to landless campesinos. (Communism is a political theory that aims, in part, to end economic injustice by state control of farms and other businesses.)

In 1931 General Maximiliano Hernández Martínez seized power. His brutal dictatorship crushed campesinos' hopes of equality. President Hernández also ended the oligarchy's political leadership. He introduced some advantages, such as schools, to the country. But the changes mainly benefited the wealthy. In 1944 a revolution by students and soldiers overthrew Hernández.

THE MASSACRE

By 1930 coffee plantations took up so much land in western El Salvador that campesinos didn't have enough cropland to survive. Coffee pickers organized to demand reforms. With the help of communist leader Augustín Farabundo Martí, they planned an uprising. In 1932 the campesinos rose in revolt and killed one hundred soldiers and landowners. General Hernández ordered the National Guard to put down the revolt. They machine-gunned entire villages and attacked rural people in the west for weeks, killing up to thirty thousand men, women, and children. Salvadorans call the event *la matanza*, which means "the massacre."

A series of military presidents ruled El Salvador for the next fifty years. Each supported the wealthy landowners and merchants. The social system remained unequal. A new constitution in 1950, however, gave Salvadoran women the right to vote.

Alliances and Clashes

El Salvador became a leader in the formation of the Central American Common Market (CACM). In a historic move, in 1960 five countries (El Salvador, Guatemala, Honduras, Nicaragua, and Costa Rica) agreed to open their markets to one another. El Salvador was quick to expand its factories to produce goods for the market.

El Salvador's presidency remained in the hands of the military. Leaders rigged elections to guarantee their power. Starting in 1960, the Christian Democratic Party (PDC, its Spanish initials) opposed the military party. The PDC steadily grew in popular support.

With the success of the CACM, El Salvador enjoyed economic progress. The introduction of sugarcane and cotton farming brought money into the country. The government spent the money on industrial improvements, including building dams and power plants on the Lempa River.

In 1962 Salvadoran university students were so fed up with corrupt elections that they nominated a donkey for president.

In the 1960s, El Salvador became a leader in promoting the Alliance for Progress. The United States and Latin American countries used the alliance to speed growth. With foreign loans and U.S. aid, El Salvador's government created new industries. The upper classes benefited from the boom. They no longer relied as much on landowning and coffee growing. With a more progressive attitude, the nation's leaders also sought to meet the needs of its people. Some made efforts to improve housing, education, and health care.

El Salvador's economic growth, however, was not enough to meet the demands of its rapidly growing population. Many people were unable to find work or farmland in their own country. Over the course of several years, about 300,000 Salvadorans emigrated to Honduras, often illegally.

In early 1969, the Honduran government began to speak out against the Salvadoran "invasion" of Honduran territory. Hondurans saw the Salvadorans as an economic threat. Along with land issues, the two countries had long disagreed about their border. The matter became a crisis when Honduras passed laws that would take away the land of

During the **1969 war between El Salvador and Honduras,** Honduran troops *(left)* find the dead bodies of Salvadoran soldiers. This war was also known as the Soccer War. That year, El Salvador and Honduras had competed in playoffs for the World Cup, an international soccer competition. The beginning of the war was sparked by riots after a hotly contested game.

illegal immigrants. In response, Salvadoran troops invaded Honduras in July 1969. The ensuing war lasted four days. It left two thousand people dead and four thousand wounded.

For El Salvador, the cost of the brief war was high. The return of emigrants swelled El Salvador's landless class to 41 percent of the rural population. The war also led to the end of the common market.

The Troubled 1970s

During the 1970s, El Salvador's economy sank. When the CACM failed, wealthy Salvadorans and foreign businesses invested their money elsewhere, mainly in the United States. After El Salvador's corrupt 1972 presidential election, protestors demanded work and land for the poor. The military crushed the protests. People who supported reform by democratic means grew frustrated. Some began to support the idea of armed uprisings to reform the country.

The Catholic Church in El Salvador had traditionally supported conservative regimes. But during this era, it began to preach reforms for the lives of poor people. In a movement called liberation theology, some priests and nuns helped oppressed Salvadorans organize into political groups. Many revolutionary leaders arose from these groups. The military continued to dominate government. A new group called the National Democratic Organization (ORDEN, its Spanish initials) worked with the National Guard to support the government. This right-wing (conservative) terrorist group began to threaten and kill people who supported political change.

The terms *right wing* and *left wing* come from the French Revolution (1789–1799). At that time, liberal lawmakers who wanted extreme reforms sat on the left wing, or side, of the legislature. Conservatives who wanted to keep things the same sat on the right side.

During the 1970s, spokespeople who opposed the government drew large crowds. Membership in left wing (reform) groups grew. Members came from a wide range of society, including students, trade union members, campesinos, and women.

Guerrilla groups formed to fight for reforms. (Guerrillas are rebels who fight in small bands and use tactics such as hit-and-run strikes.) Leftists began to kidnap businesspeople for ransom money to fund their activities. They also assassinated some right-wing politicians. Fraud and violence marked the elections of 1977. In 1979 the success of a communist revolution in Nicaragua inspired Salvadoran rebels. They hoped they too might overthrow their corrupt government.

◗ Civil War

By 1980 the violence between left-wing and right-wing groups had spiraled out of control. Civil war broke out between the military government and rebel groups. In what came to be called a dirty war, both sides dealt out fear and violent death. Army-backed death squads terrorized, tortured, and murdered anyone they thought might oppose the government. Every morning, citizens found mutilated bodies dumped on the streets of San Salvador.

Among the Catholic priests who spoke out for the poor and against the death squads was Oscar Arnulfo Romero y Galdames. He was the archbishop (high church official) of San Salvador. In March 1980, he gave what became a famous radio sermon. He addressed El Salvador's soldiers, begging them to disobey orders to kill their own people. The next day, a pro-government assassin murdered Romero during a church service. The murder shocked the nation and the world. About 250,000 people gathered for the archbishop's funeral at San Salvador's cathedral. Soldiers fired into the crowd, killing 30 people.

Oscar Arnulfo Romero y Galdames had been nominated for the Nobel Peace Prize in 1979. (Mother Teresa of India received the prize that year.) His assassination on March 24, 1980, was world news.

Following the assassination, El Salvador's leading rebel groups united into one group–the FMLN (Farabundo Martí National Liberation Front). They named it after the leader of the 1932 campesino uprising. Politicians who supported reform began to support the armed FMLN.

Nine months after Romero's murder, another atrocity drew the United States's attention to El Salvador. Government soldiers raped and murdered four American churchwomen who were helping war victims in El Salvador. The next month, the assassination of two American land-reform advisers increased U.S. president Jimmy Carter's concern. He briefly cut off aid to El Salvador. However, human rights abuses continued as before.

One of the conflict's principal figures was José Napoleón Duarte. The ruling junta (group in power) appointed him president of El Salvador in December 1980. An elected assembly wrote a new constitution. But the civil war continued raging. The military carried out scorched-earth (complete destruction) operations in rural

WOMEN AT WAR

Many Salvadoran women worked and fought for a better society during the civil war. Rebecca Palacios was a member of the FMLN. In an interview, she explained that her motivation was "rooted in the fact that the Salvadoran people have shown that they are no longer willing to be anybody's slave. The people have an immense longing for democracy. . . . So if my people, an illiterate, poor, underdeveloped people, have this kind of spirit to keep on struggling and moving forward, in spite of what has been done to them, in spite of the bombings, in spite of the massacres, . . . then I have absolute confidence that this people has the. . . strength capable of changing the destiny of our country."

—from *The Hour of the Poor, the Hour of Women: Salvadoran Women Speak*, edited by Renny Golden, p. 178

Read more about El Salvador's civil war and subsequent struggles to achieve and hold on to peace for all Salvadorans. Visit www.vgsbooks.com for links.

areas where rebel groups dominated. In 1981 soldiers machine-gunned hundreds of unarmed campesinos in the village of El Mozote. Salvadorans count this event as one of the worst atrocities of the civil war.

Duarte was elected president in 1984. He counted on strong support from U.S. president Ronald Reagan. The United States supplied the Salvadoran military with arms, financial aid, and advisers. Salvadoran troops received training at American army bases. U.S. military aid strengthened the powerful Salvadoran army. Especially important was the supply of U.S. air power. The Salvadoran air force used U.S. helicopters and planes to bomb rebel targets.

Fiercely anticommunist, Reagan believed that he was fighting the spread of communism in Latin America. Communist nations Cuba and Nicaragua supported the FMLN. The Soviet Union (a union of republics including Russia)—the world's communist superpower—backed Cuba's aid.

In return for its assistance, the United States insisted that the Salvadoran government stop violations of human rights and begin land reform. Salvadoran lawmakers did craft a land-reform program. It was to give land to 150,000 campesinos. However, due to right-wing opposition, fewer than 1,000 people actually received land.

The U.S.-backed military weakened the FMLN. The guerrillas destroyed bridges, coffee estates, and buses to weaken the government. The military responded with air strikes to the rural areas where guerrillas operated. Their bombs destroyed livestock and crops, as well as killing humans. The people who suffered most were the campesinos. Therefore, many stopped supporting or were too afraid to support the FMLN. Gradually the Salvadoran army began to regain rebel-held areas.

Negotiations for peace between the two sides kept failing. Each side made impossible demands and would not compromise. During this period, several natural disasters also struck El Salvador. They included an earthquake in 1986, a hurricane in 1988, and severe drought during several growing seasons.

Duarte's term ended in 1989. A wealthy coffee grower named Alfredo Cristiani succeeded Duarte. Cristiani was the head of the right-wing Nationalist Republican Alliance (ARENA). He made sweeping reforms in the Salvadoran economy and began negotiations with the FMLN. The

ARENA government continued to receive weapons, training, and money from the United States. U.S. aid totaled $6 billion during the civil war.

By 1989 external and internal pressures had weakened the Soviet Union. Without its backing, communist nations cut their military supplies to El Salvador. Tensions between the United States and communist nations began to relax. That year the FMLN launched a final push against the military. They occupied parts of San Salvador for several days. In retaliation, in the early hours of November 16, 1989, death squad members murdered six pro-reform priests, their housekeeper, and her teenage daughter. No one was winning the war.

▶ Peacetime

Both sides of the civil war were tired of the violence. The fighting had reached a stalemate. In the early 1990s, the United Nations (UN, an international peacekeeping organization) assembled both sides for peace talks. Representatives of the warring sides signed a final Peace Accords in Chapultepec, Mexico, on January 16, 1992. The FMLN agreed to lay down its arms and rejoin the civilian population. The government agreed to end its support of death squads and to support land reform. Both sides agreed to participate in peaceful democratic elections in two years. The UN set up a mission to guide the peace process.

Thousands of Salvadorans took to the streets to celebrate the end of twelve years of bloodshed. In a country of only 7 million people, more than 75,000 Salvadorans had lost their lives. Many more were

In **celebration of the January 16, 1992, peace treaty,** two women *(left)* release doves in San Salvador's central plaza.

wounded. Besides loss of life and widespread destruction, the civil war cost the nation more than $1 billion. An estimated two million Salvadorans fled their country during the war or became refugees in their own country. Many of them emigrated to the United States, often illegally.

The Peace Accords set up new institutions to build a democratic society. Land-reform laws were an important part of the accords. A government agency was set up to redistribute land. It soon ran into serious problems, however. As a result, most campesinos remained landless. More successfully, a police force replaced the hated and feared National Guard. The government and the military also fired people who had abused human rights.

El Salvador held its first postwar elections on March 20, 1994. The ARENA leader Armando Calderon Sol won the presidency. A coalition (multiparty group) of leftist parties, including the FMLN, won some seats in the Salvadoran legislature. Sol announced that the Peace Accords' changes were mostly in place.

Peacetime did not stop all violence, however. In the aftermath of war, crime swept the country. With families and traditional ways of life

Former FMLN guerrillas celebrate their peace treaty with the Salvadoran government. The 1992 treaty made the FMLN a government-recognized political party.

destroyed, thousands of young men joined violent gangs.

In 1998 Hurricane Mitch slammed into El Salvador. Winds up to 180 miles (290 km) per hour tore apart buildings. The hurricane caused extreme rainfall that led to widespread floods and landslides. More than three hundred people were killed.

In 1999 the ARENA candidate once again won the presidential election. President Francisco Flores Perez focused on improving El Salvador's economy. The country made progress repairing Hurricane Mitch damage.

The Twenty-First Century

On January 1, 2001, El Salvador adopted the United States dollar as its main form of currency. The move was meant to stabilize the economy. Two weeks later, a massive earthquake struck. Landslides of mud crushed people, smashed cars, and ripped apart houses. One month later, another earthquake shook the country. The quakes killed two thousand people and injured eight thousand. They damaged or destroyed 25 percent of Salvadorans' homes, leaving 1.5 million people without shelter. The cost of the damage was almost $2 billion. Later in the year, a drought destroyed 80 percent of the country's crops. Famine struck the countryside.

In 2002 Salvadorans celebrated the tenth anniversary of the end of the civil war. Despite many challenges, peace and democracy had taken root in the country. President Flores marked the event in a mountain village that was once a guerrilla stronghold. That year, U.S. president George W. Bush met with Central American presidents in El Salvador. The United States is El Salvador's main trading partner. Bush promoted free trade (trade without taxes) between the United States and Central America.

Under ARENA leadership, El Salvador's economy improved. Nonetheless, the FMLN won a majority of seats in the legislature in 2003. Salvadorans also chose an FMLN candidate as mayor of San Salvador. That same year, President Flores sent 360 Salvadoran troops to Iraq. They joined a U.S.-led coalition of forces that removed Iraq's dictator, Saddam Hussein, from power.

A LETHAL LEGACY

Though El Salvador does not make guns, it has more weapons per person than most countries in the world. Arms from El Salvador's civil war are still in use. Once supplied by foreign countries, assault rifles are long lasting. The weapons were designed for hard use in bad weather. The AK-47 rifle, for instance, can be buried in mud and still work afterward. Criminals gather and resell the guns. Sometimes they sell them to other countries where there is high demand for guns.

In 2004 voters chose Elías Antonio "Tony" Saca for president. Ana Vilma de Escobar became El Salvador's first woman vice president. Saca is the fourth president in a row from the ARENA party. During the civil war, ARENA had supported the death squads. But Saca—only thirty-nine years old—had not been involved in the civil war. He promised to cooperate with other political parties, to strengthen ties with the United Sates, and to crack down on gang crime.

While offering a fresh face, Saca faces ongoing problems in El Salvador. Almost 60 percent of the population lives in poverty. Thousands of gang members engage in street crime. Nevertheless, El Salvador's government operates with a basic respect for civil and human rights.

One year after Saca's election, natural disasters struck the country yet again. The Santa Ana Volcano erupted, killing two people and causing thousands to flee. Tropical Storm Stan swept the coast a few days later, killing many people.

El Salvador's highest volcano, Santa Ana, erupted in October 2005. The volcano spat burning rocks as far as 1 mile (1.6 km) from its crater. Villagers reported lava rocks as big as cows.

In 2006 El Salvador became the first Central American country to implement the Central America Free Trade Agreement (CAFTA) with the United States. The agreement makes trade between the nations easier. The government hopes CAFTA will reduce poverty, foster economic development, and strengthen democracy in El Salvador. Critics, however, are concerned that free trade does not protect workers' rights and the environment. That same year, El Salvador and Honduras settled the border dispute they had fought over in 1969.

Government

El Salvador is a democratic republic operating under a 1983 constitution. This document, replacing the constitution of 1962, provides for a three-part governmental system. The system consists of executive, legislative, and judicial branches. All people 18 years and older are eligible to vote.

Executive power is held by a president, who serves a five-year term. The president cannot serve two terms in a row. The unicameral (one-house) legislative body is called the National Assembly. Citizens elect its eighty-four representatives for three-year terms. An independent Supreme Court exercises judicial authority. The legislature nominates its members. In 1996 postwar constitutional reforms improved the justice system.

For administrative purposes, the country is divided into fourteen departments. Each has a regional capital. The central government appoints the department governors to four-year terms. In turn, the departments are separated into districts called *municipios* (municipalities).

Elías Antonio Saca *(left)* takes the oath of office as the president of El Salvador on June 1, 2004. The president serves a five-year term.

THE PEOPLE

El Salvador is home to 7 million people. With 862 people per square mile (333 per sq. km), it is the most densely populated country in Central America. El Salvador is also one of the fastest-growing nations in the Americas. A Salvadoran woman will give birth to an average of 3 children during her life. About 36 percent of the country's population is under the age of fifteen. The large number of young women entering childbearing years guarantees that the population will continue to grow. Experts estimate that El Salvador's population will reach 9.1 million people by 2025.

El Salvador's social welfare system is not able to handle the needs of all the people. Where and how future generations will live is a question that concerns Salvadorans. The press of people is most acutely felt in the Central Highlands. The movement of people from rural to urban areas during the civil war led to the creation of large slums. Migrants continue to move from the countryside to the cities.

One way to look at the well-being of a country's people is to con-

sult the United Nations' Human Development Index (HDI). The UN ranks the human development of 177 countries. It measures the prospects of a person in a particular country having a long, healthy life with education and a good standard of living. El Salvador ranks 103 out of 177 countries. It places a little better than its neighbors Honduras (115) and Guatemala (121). But it is far below the Middle American countries of Costa Rica (45) and Mexico (53). The HDI of the United States is 8.

Ethnic Groups

The mixing of different ethnic groups over many centuries has created a Salvadoran population that is 92 percent mestizo. People of unmixed European (mostly Spanish) descent make up 5 percent of the population. The remaining 3 percent are descendants of El Salvador's indigenous people. They are mostly Pipil, the largest group at the time of the Spanish conquest.

Indigenous people in El Salavdor mostly blend into mainstream culture. The Spanish conquerors violently suppressed native customs in El Salvador. During the 1932 massacre, government troops especially targeted indigenous people. Therefore, the surviving native people gave up ways of life that exposed them to danger, such as traditional clothing. Only a very few still follow the ways of their ancestors. They live mostly in the southwestern highlands along the Guatemalan border. Some still speak the ancient Nahuatl language. But most Salvadorans speak Spanish, El Salvador's official language.

El Salvador's small but powerful minority of European descent is centered in San Salvador. Some of the country's prominent families trace their lineage to the Spanish conquerors. The so-called Fourteen Families of colonial times still control much of the economy, but they number closer to two hundred elite families. Well-educated and well-traveled, San Salvador's ruling elite is cosmopolitan in taste and outlook.

GANG LIFE

Violent gangs plague El Salvador. Officials estimate that gang members number ten thousand. Young Salvadoran men began many of the gangs during the 1980s, while living in Los Angeles, California. In the early 1990s, the U.S. government sent hundreds of the gang members back to El Salvador, where they caused a crime wave. The murder rate in San Salvador rose to 9 per day. Rival gangs engage in turf wars, and murder is one of the duties of gang membership. Gangs provide their members with a place to belong and a strict code of behavior. Breaking gang codes leads to punishment, including death. Few gang members live to be older than thirty.

◉ Ways of Life

Salvadorans are generally serious and hardworking. They tend to be less openly emotional than other Central American peoples. Family ties in El Salvador are strong. Often two or three generations of a family live under the same roof. Businesses often operate through networks of family members.

While Salvadorans share many values, El Salvador is far from being a united country. The divisions are especially clear in the differences between city and country life. Much of San Salvador, for instance, feels like an American city, with shopping malls and fast-food restaurants. Most people live in apartments, though poor neighborhoods of shacks exist. Wealthy people live in large, modern houses, often behind high walls.

Despite urbanization, 41 percent of Salvadorans lead rural lives on small farms or in villages. Barely two hours from the capital, the rural way of life has changed little in centuries. Dirt roads are pitted with potholes. People live in small villages of wattle and daub or adobe huts. They make their wattle and daub huts from interwoven branches covered with mud. Adobe houses are made of sun-dried clay bricks. Most houses have dirt floors. Families living together often include grandparents, aunts, uncles, and cousins.

Many rural people, including children, work for plantation owners. Farmers walk or take buses or trucks early in the morning to work. They also tend their own small cornfields around the villages. They are able to grow just enough to feed their families. Women grind corn by hand and use it to make tortillas. They cook over a fire stove, with wood they gather. Nearly one-quarter of rural people are without clean drinking water and sanitation in their homes. Many do not have electricity, plumbing, or telephones. Young people face the choice of continuing this life or leaving to find work. Many go to big cities or enter the United States, joining more than 1 million Salvadorans already in that country.

This **traditional adobe house in a tiny village near Sonsonate** has a wooden lean-to that shades its outdoor kitchen.

Machismo, or an extreme pride in being male, is strong in El Salvador. Men are in charge at all levels. They dominate the country's government and businesses. Violence against women is common. The government established the Institute for the Development of Women to address the plight of women who suffer from abuse in the home.

Women's participation in the civil war empowered many to speak out against injustice in their own lives. They are leaders, for instance, in promoting family planning and improved health care. Groups such as Women for Dignity and Life (DIGNAS) work to overcome the disadvantages women face. The vice president of El Salvador is a woman, and women make up 11 percent of the country's legislature. They are making slow progress in reaching economic, social, and political equality.

Education

El Salvador had no public education system until the mid-1800s. In the 1980s, a generation of children grew up with little education because of the civil war. Literacy rates demonstrate that young people have benefited from better opportunities for education since 1992. Only 80 percent of El Salvador's overall population is literate, or able to read and write a basic sentence. But among people 15 to 24 years old, the rate rises to 89 percent. The literacy rate is slightly lower for women than for men. Families are more likely to keep girls home to help with the work.

Education is free and compulsory (legally required) through ninth grade. There are more than 5,000 grade schools in El Salvador. About 85 percent of Salvadoran children attend grade school. However, there are only about 800 high schools. Almost all of them are in cities. Only about 20 percent of Salvadorans graduate from high school. The Ministry of Education is working to reform and expand high school education.

Children from wealthy families may attend private, secular (nonreligious) schools. These schools

GENETIC TESTING REUNITES FAMILIES

The civil war tore apart thousands of families. Lost, orphaned, or kidnapped children were given or sold into adoption in El Salvador and abroad. The group Salvadoran Association in Search of Missing Children works to reunite relatives separated years ago. With the help of the University of California, DNA is being used to confirm family relationships. By 2007 the organization had used genetic testing to match three hundred children—now young adults—with their birth families.

At **school in El Vado,** lively kindergartners eat lunch together. Find out more about education, housing, and health in El Salvador. Go to www.vgsbooks.com for links.

provide excellent educations to prepare children for professional careers. In these schools, English is the preferred language. Catholic and evangelical churches also run private schools.

El Salvador has three universities and close to thirty small technical schools and colleges. The University of El Salvador—the first in the country—was founded in 1841. The largest university in the country, it accommodates 30,000 students. War and earthquakes have damaged many of the university's buildings. The university does not have the money to rebuild all of its facilities. Nonetheless, it offers a full range of courses in many fields. Students study business, education, science, and technology. Even with many smaller colleges, El Salvador's need for higher education exceeds available space. Only 1 percent of Salvadorans complete a college degree. Wealthy families commonly send their children to universities in the United States and Europe.

One of the areas of study at the University of El Salvador is volcanology, or the science of volcanoes.

Lack of adequate schooling, especially in rural areas, remains a primary cause of discontent among Salvadorans. The nation does not have enough teachers or schools. Many children do not go to school at all or only for a few years. To be competitive in the world economy, El Salvador needs to improve its educational system. The government is addressing the challenge. It spends more than 13 percent of its budget on education. It also funds the Healthy Schools program to give every schoolchild a proper diet and health care.

▶ Health

Salvadorans' average life expectancy of 70 years—73 for women and 67 for men—marks an improvement for the country since the 1980s. It is close to Central America's life expectancy of 74 years. The average for northern America (Canada and the United States) is 78 years. El Salvador's infant mortality rate (numbers of babies who die before their first birthday) is 25 deaths out of every 1,000 live births. This figure is about average for Central America. Northern America averages 7 deaths per 1,000 babies.

El Salvador's government provides health care through hospitals and many local clinics. However, most of these are located in urban areas. Rural areas are underserved. About 25 percent of the population does not have access to health services. Salvadorans who can afford it can pay for private medical care.

Some Salvadorans seek medical advice from *curanderos*. These natural healers practice native traditions, especially in the countryside. Curanderos may perform rituals or prescribe natural herbal remedies. Some people believe they possess magical powers.

Health care in El Salvador has greatly improved since 1992. However, poverty, overpopulation, and natural disasters burden El Salvador's health care system. Many people suffer from diseases linked to poor diet and unsanitary living conditions. Only 66 percent of rural dwellers and 91 percent of those living in urban areas have clean drinking water at home. Open sewage is a constant health threat. During the yearly rainy season, filth and garbage gets washed into the drinking water system. This spread of germs leads to a high rate of diarrhea. While not a serious threat to healthy adults, diarrhea is the leading cause of death in children under age five. The country also continues to experience outbreaks of cholera. Dirty drinking water causes this deadly disease. However, successful programs have reduced

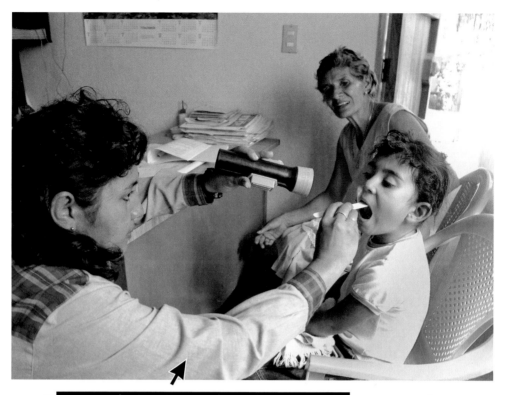

At **a community health center in San Francisco Javier,** a nurse examines a child.

threats from tropical diseases such as malaria, spread by mosquitoes. El Salvador's rate of HIV/AIDS (human immunodeficiency virus/ acquired immunodeficiency syndrome) is 0.9 percent.

In 2002 Salvadoran health care workers, including hundreds of doctors, went on strike. They opposed the government's plan to privatize (sell to private owners) health care. That is, the government planned to stop providing national health care. Many Salvadorans believed that a for-profit system would make health care even less available to poor people. In response to the strike, the government outlawed the privatization of health care. The new law emphasizes quality health care for all Salvadorans, near their home, whether or not they are able to pay.

CULTURAL LIFE

Spanish traditions long dominated El Salvador's culture, and Spanish is the official language. However, native culture lingers in the storytelling, art, and religion of the nation. Modern artists and musicians often use Mayan and Pipil symbols and myths in their creative work. The civil war was a time of fear and destruction, and artistic expression suffered. Since 1992 the spirit of peace and restoration has led to a renewal of Salvadoran creativity. American cultural influences also shape modern El Salvador. Especially in big cities, Salvadoran culture reflects the United States in everything from television shows and computer games to fast-food restaurants and shopping malls.

◉ Literature

El Salvador has a rich history of oral storytelling that dates back to the original inhabitants. Especially in rural areas, people tell tales that involve animals and heroes with supernatural powers. Many of these stories have pre-Spanish roots.

El Salvador has produced many writers since its independence in 1821. José Batres y Montúfar (1809–1844) was the country's first nineteenth-century writer of note. In his poetry, he wrote of the anguish of life during the late colonial period. Other authors also wrote in the Romantic style. This style emphasized nature and the plight of common people. The most famous Romantic-era poet was Juan José Cañas (1826–1918). He spent much of his life abroad and wrote nostalgically of his homeland. He also composed El Salvador's national anthem.

Probably the giant of Salvadoran literature was Francisco Gavidia (1863–1955). He was a poet, essayist, and playwright. Critics consider him the most important Salvadoran writer of his time. His most important poem was "To Central America." In it, he condemned tyranny and expressed faith in the unity of Central American countries.

Politics have often been a force in Salvadoran literature. After the 1932 massacre of campesinos, a handful of writers protested the military regime in their writing. The most important literary figure from that era is Salvador Salazar Arrué (1899–1975). He signed his novels, short stories, and paintings with the alias Salarrué. He took a leading role in making the short-story form popular in Central America. Blending magic and spirituality, Salarrué portrayed the inner lives of El Salvador's rural people. His most famous book is *Cuentos de barro* (Tales of Mud, 1934). Other writers followed in his footsteps. The novelist Alberto Rivas Bonilla (1891–1985) wrote one of El Salvador's best-loved novels, *Andanzas y malandanzas* (Adventures and Misadventures, 1936). This colorful tale, supposedly about a dog's life, is really a commentary on life in El Salvador.

Many poets represent El Salvador. Claudia Lars (1899–1974) is among the most outstanding. Her collection *Nuestro pulsante Mundo* (Our Pulsating World, 1969) reflects her interests, ranging from rock music to space exploration.

Writers expressed their frustration at the military regime during the 1970s. Roque Dalton (1935–1975) used his pen to call for armed struggle against the regime. The government banned his books and put him in prison. Using humor as well as despair, Dalton captured the history of his suffering country with his words. Fellow rebels suspected him of being a spy, however, and executed him.

The civil war was not a fertile time for Salvadoran literature. A number of promising writers lost their lives. Dalton's contemporary Manlio Argueta (b. 1935) continued to write about liberation, agony, and social responsibility. But he wrote from exile in Costa Rica. Another famous writer, Claribel Alegría (b. 1924), also left the country. She has written more than thirty works of novels, nonfiction, and poetry. Alegría's most powerful writings show the ugliness of human cruelty. In her long poem *La Mujer del río Sumpul* (The Woman of the Sumpul River, 1987), Alegría imagines the voices of victims during one of the war's massacres.

Between 1979 and 1990, author and playwright Mario Bencastro wrote a collection

Manlio Argueta's novel *Un dia en la vida* (*One Day of Life*, 1980) follows the day of a peasant family caught up in the terrors of the civil war. Because the story exposed military brutality, the government banned the book in the 1980s. But it became a best-seller abroad, in translation. In 2000 Modern Library placed it fifth in a list of the one hundred best Latin American novels of the twentieth century. Students in modern El Salvador study the book in school.

of short stories. They appeared in 1993 in English with the title *The Tree of Life: Stories of Civil War.* His novel for young adults, *Viaje a la tierra del abuelo* (Trip to Grandfather's Land, 2004) tells the story of a teenager in Los Angeles who returns to El Salvador to bury his grandfather.

Peacetime brought a return of literary freedom to El Salvador. Argueta returned home and continued writing. Among his postwar novels is *Milagro de la paz* (The Miracle of Peace, 1994). Horacio Castellanos Moya is the most prominent of El Salvador's postwar writers. He gained fame with the 1997 publication of his dark novel *El asco* (Disgust). His writings portray the complexities of life and politics in Central America. His novel *El arma en el hombre* (The Weapon in Man, 2002), for instance, is about a death-squad member after the end of the civil war.

Media and Film

El Salvador's constitution guarantees freedom of the press. Private owners dominate Salvadoran media. The country publishes four daily national newspapers. Journalists regularly criticize the government and freely report on opposition activities. Radio is a popular form of communication. San Salvador alone hosts about seventy radio stations. Well-off Salvadorans across much of the country get international TV channels through cable and satellite dishes.

A man catches up on the day's national news while waiting for a bus in San Salvador. Four daily newspapers are published in El Salvador.

El Salvador produces few films. Cero a la Izquierda, a collective of Salvadoran filmmakers, made documentaries during the civil war. *The Decision to Win* (1982) portrayed the guerrillas' fierce determination. The 2004 Mexican film *Innocent Voices* retells the story of the war through the eyes of an eleven-year-old boy. Salvadoran Oscar Torres cowrote the script, based on his own life. He joined the FMLN when he was twelve and later escaped to the United States.

Music and Dance

Long before the Spanish conquest, music played an important part in Salvadoran life. Archaeologists have found various kinds of musical instruments—whistles with several tones; pipes with as many as six finger holes; and drums of wood or clay called *huehuetls,* originally covered with deerskin. The marimba, a wooden xylophone, also has a long history and is still played.

Traditional songs include religious music, songs for festival days, and themes of rural life. Folk songs sometimes make fun of the rich and powerful. Modern popular music has its roots in Spanish, Cuban, and Mexican music. Salvadoran bands frequently play a bouncy style called *cumbia,* originally from Colombia, with a repetitive beat.

A musician in Panchimalco shows how to play a traditional **Salvadoran musical instrument** made from a gourd.

Some Salvadoran musicians make a name for themselves in the United States. Brothers Victor and Johnny Lopez are a Spanish-language rap duo called Crooked Stilo. Born in El Salvador, the brothers live in Los Angeles. Blending hip-hop with Latin rhythms, they released their third album, *Retrosalo,* in 2005.

Traditional dance is a blend of Spanish and indigenous influences. On festival days, people in colorful costumes act out tales in song and dance. Decorated wooden masks represent stock characters, such as a fool with a monkey face.

Salvadoran composers have been numerous. In 1860 José Escolástico Andrino became the country's first composer. He wrote church music, symphonies, and one opera. He also formed the first symphonic orchestra. The twentieth-century composers Wenceslao García and María Mendoza de Baratta both emphasize Indian themes. Two composers both born in 1968—Carlos Mendizabal and Carlos Colon Quintana—are promising in the twenty-first century.

El Salvador's fine National Symphonic Orchestra enjoys funding from both government and private sources. Under the baton of distinguished directors, the orchestra is a credit to the cultural life of the country.

Folk Art and Painting

Salvadorans are famous for their lively folk art, especially ceramics. Brightly painted clay objects often use native and peasant symbols. A specialty is *sorpresas* (surprises)—little painted figures under a walnut-sized clay shell. Wood carvers create masks, Spanish riders, religious items, and traditional peasant dolls.

Painting is the most important modern art in El Salvador, with a long history of excellence. A Salvadoran national school of painting developed in the early twentieth century. Notable painters of this school were Juan Francisco Cisneros and Miguel Ortíz Villacorta. Author Salarrué was one of El Salvador's most original painters. His experimental art displays the same interest in the inner life that his stories do. He experimented with "automatic" painting, for instance, letting his hand paint without interference from his conscious mind.

Notable among modern painters is José Mejía Vides (b. 1923). He depicts the lives of ordinary people and the villages of his home country. The paintings of Noé Canjura (1924–1970) are full of social and religious themes, such as his painting *Indian Christ.* The vibrant and colorful art of Fernando Llort (b. 1949) is rooted in folk traditions. In the 1970s, Llort founded an art center at La Palma, Chalatenango. With his support, the artisans of La Palma have become well known.

Religion

The constitution of El Salvador guarantees freedom of religion. The country's history as a colony of Roman Catholic Spain left El Salvador a largely Catholic nation. Remnants of traditional native religion survived by blending into Catholic practices. The Catholic Church claims about 83 percent of the population, though a large percentage do not attend church regularly. The other 17 percent are mostly members of Protestant (non-Catholic) Christian churches. Evangelical churches actively preach and work in El Salvador. They reach out with programs to help those who live in poverty. There are also small communities of members of the Church of Jesus Christ of Latter-day Saints (Mormons), Jews, and Muslims. A very small part of the population practices a native religion.

The involvement of Catholic leaders in politics made the church a target of violence during the 1980s. Catholic clergy openly criticized the nation's age-old injustices. In contrast to the conservative Church, which preached acceptance, the clergy developed liberation theology. Through this teaching, they encouraged ordinary people to actively create a just society. Opponents accused the Church of meddling in politics and of dividing the nation's people. These conflicts led to harassment and even murder of clergy and other Catholics working for change.

During these troubled times, many Salvadorans turned to Protestant evangelical churches. At first, most Protestant churchgoers were from poor, rural areas where the Catholic clergy had fled. By the mid-1990s, however, wealthier professionals such as lawyers and doctors had joined the evangelical churches. In the twenty-first century, close to one out of every five Salvadorans is Protestant.

Find out more about El Salvador's culture—its religions, art, music, dance, sports, and food. Go to www.vgsbooks.com for links.

Holidays and Festivals

El Salvador's calendar is full of festivals. May 1 is International Labor Day. Salvadorans celebrate independence from Spain on September 15. Yearly parades mark the 1821 event. But most holidays are religious celebrations. Government offices close on religious holidays.

El Salvador's most important national festival falls on August 6. It honors the nation's patron (special protector) saint: Jesus as El Salvador del Mundo—the "Holy Savior of the World." The name of the country comes from this Spanish title. Celebrations begin the week before August 6. A wooden image of Christ, carved in 1777, is paraded through the streets of

San Salvador. The festival includes sports events—soccer games, bicycle races, and boxing matches. Operators of Ferris wheels and merry-go-rounds do a thriving business at this time. The regional governor crowns a Queen of the August Fair.

In rural areas, each village celebrates its own patron saint. These yearly events are lively affairs. Fireworks, band concerts, the breaking of piñatas (candy-filled papier-mâché figures), street markets, and religious ceremonies occur with as much pomp as possible. These traditional celebrations and rituals have an important place in national life.

During the week before Christmas, groups of children take part in *las posadas*, as in other Latin American countries. The children wear costumes and go from door to door seeking shelter for baby Jesus. A feast awaits them at the end of their search. Salvadorans also celebrate Holy Week before Easter. Government offices and other workplaces close for much of the week.

For this **playful traditional skit for Holy Week in Texistepeque,** the masked men dressed in red represent devils.

Aspiring **young soccer players practice their sport in a local graveyard** in Antiguo Cuscatlán.

Sports and Recreation

Soccer, called *fútbol* (football) in El Salvador, is the country's national sport. El Salvador's national team has competed in the World Cup twice—in 1970 and 1982. Basketball, baseball, volleyball, boxing, and tennis are also popular sports. Thousands of fans follow automobile racing. The Formula One auto racecourse outside San Salvador holds 100,000 spectators. Along the coast, people enjoy swimming, water skiing, and surfing. Some well-off Salvadorans spend weekends at ocean resorts.

Family is the most important social unit in El Salvador. Many people have little time for leisure, but Salvadorans like to socialize with family and friends in the evenings when the day cools off.

Food

The diet of most Salvadorans is similar to that of other Latin Americans. Breakfast is simply coffee with milk and rolls. Lunch is the main meal, and dinner is a lighter meal. Corn tortillas and stewed or fried beans are staples. Rice and vegetables may accompany these simple foods. Less commonly seen are meat, cheese, poultry, and fish. Particularly in rural areas, the diet is heavy on starches. As a result, many people there are not well nourished.

In urban areas, the diet is more varied. San Salvador is known for its fine restaurants. Many people buy their fresh fruits and vegetables at open-air markets. City supermarkets offer a broad range of foods. Shrimp, lobster, swordfish, and other seafood caught in the Pacific provide excellent eating.

Almost everybody eats *pupusas*—stuffed, flat cornmeal cakes that are the national specialty. Favorite fillings include beans, crispy pork

A vendor prepares **pupusas,** stuffed cornmeal patties, in the town of Juayua.

skins, or cheese with spices. Pumpkin, shrimp, and fish are other fillings. *Curtido*, a kind of coleslaw, accompanies pupusas. *Pupuserías*, shops that offer these foods, are common all over El Salvador.

Candy makers in El Salvador are famous for their specialties. A unique creation is *dulce de camote*. This yam candy is shaped like a volcano.

Many Salvadorans have a sweet tooth. Bakers produce a wide assortment of cakes and pastries. They may fill them with pineapple jelly or sprinkle them with coconut. Street vendors sell *minuta*—crushed ice flavored with sweet syrups.

Drinks made from tropical fruits are a typical part of the Salvadoran diet. *Horchata*, made of gourd seeds and flavored with cocoa, is the most common. Mango, coconut, guava, and the tart tamarind are the base for other popular drinks. *Atol* is a popular milky looking, corn-based drink. Some rural people drink a liquor called *aguardiente*, which means "burning water."

A **popular dessert in El Salvador** is *pastel de tres leches*, or three milks cake.

CURTIDO (COLESLAW)

For a traditional meal, serve curtido with beans and rice. Flavor pinto or black beans with onion, garlic, and chili powder. Heat, and spoon over rice. Watermelon makes a good finish to the meal.

¾ cup pineapple juice

1 cup apple cider vinegar

pinch of oregano

2 tablespoons vegetable oil

1 cabbage, finely sliced

3 large carrots, grated

5 cups boiling water

1 onion, thinly sliced

1 green and 1 red bell pepper, seeded and finely chopped

pinch of oregano

2 teaspoons red chili flakes

½ teaspoon salt

1. Mix pineapple juice, apple cider vinegar, oregano, and 1 tablespoon vegetable oil in a bowl. Set aside.
2. In heat-proof bowl, cover cabbage and carrots with boiling water. Let sit 5 minutes. Drain well. Place cabbage mix in another large bowl.
3. Heat 1 tablespoon vegetable oil in a frying pan on medium heat. Fry onion, bell peppers, oregano, chili flakes, and salt for 10 minutes. Stir often. Add to the bowl with cabbage, mixing well.
4. Pour pineapple-vinegar mix over the cabbage mix. Stir well to coat all the vegetables. Serve immediately or refrigerate.

Serves 6 to 8

THE ECONOMY

El Salvador is a country of economic contrasts. On the surface, the nation has experienced impressive growth since the end of the civil war. New roads take shoppers to vast malls where they can buy imported goods. Foreign investment in *maquiladoras* (export-assembly plants) and other industries has created jobs. The 2006 free trade agreement with the United States opens up more trade between the two countries by removing taxes on imports and other barriers to trade. At the same time, El Salvador struggles with a legacy of poverty and civil war. Repairs from earthquakes and other natural disasters are very costly. The government has borrowed a lot of money from other countries to pay for reconstruction.

El Salvador's average income per person is $5,120. The average for Central America is $8,640. Northern America averages $40,980. El Salvador's income is not equally distributed. About 41 percent of Salvadorans live below the international poverty line of $2 per day.

Life in El Salvador's countryside offers little hope for the future.

Therefore, many rural people have moved to the United States. There they work doing construction, child care, and other service jobs. El Salvador's economy relies partly on remittances, or money these immigrants send home. The remittances make up 16 percent of El Salvador's gross domestic product (GDP, the value of goods and services produced in a country in a year).

Services and Tourism

Service jobs provide business, private, and public services rather than producing goods. The service sector includes jobs in government, health care, education, retail trade, banking, and tourism. Services provide 60 percent of El Salvador's GDP. Service jobs employ 66 percent of the workforce.

El Salvador's tourism industry is the main earner for the service sector. Visitors spend $425 million in the country yearly. This makes tourism the country's second-largest earner of foreign exchange (after remittances). After the 2001 earthquakes, the government spent millions of dollars promoting tourism and developing recreational and cultural activities. The country offers magnificent scenery, volcanoes, mountain lakes, and ocean beaches. El Salvador's ancient temples and ruins attract many foreign visitors. Some visitors take advantage of "ecotourism" tours. Ecotourism guides offer ways to visit rain forests without damaging the environment. Money from ecotourism is invested in protecting the land. Almost 1 million visitors arrive in El Salvador yearly. The nation's high crime rate, however, discourages some tourists. About one-third of the visitors are Salvadorans who live abroad, returning to visit family and friends.

Industry, Manufacturing, Mining, and Energy

Industry provides El Salvador with 30 percent of its GDP. The industrial sector employs 17 percent of the Salvadoran workforce. It includes jobs in manufacturing, construction, and mining.

El Salvador's industries boomed during the 1960s, when the country was part of the Central American Common Market. The outbreak of civil war brought investment in manufacturing to a halt. As factories shut down or were destroyed, thousands of laborers lost their jobs. The economy stagnated as El Salvador lost ground to its many competitors in Central America. Manufacturing began to recover after the cease-fire of 1992. Foreign companies returned. New industries began to take advantage of a free trade agreement among El Salvador, Honduras, and Guatemala.

Many of El Salvador's industries are closely tied to agriculture. Food processing, including the production of refined sugar and ground coffee, make up the largest manufacturing sector. The textile industry uses locally grown cotton and cloth dyed in El Salvador. Other important products are beverages, chemicals, fertilizer, and furniture.

Maquiladoras are export-assembly factories. These factories import raw materials and machines to El Salvador. In the factories, Salvadoran workers assemble goods, mostly cutting and sewing clothes. Maquiladoras operate in free enterprise zones—an area where all the labor and materials are tax-free. This makes them attractive to foreign investors. El Salvador has fifteen free enterprise zones. Maquiladoras first began exporting to the United States, which dropped import duties (taxes) on clothing and textiles. Maquiladoras employ mostly women who often labor under poor working conditions for little pay. El Salvador poorly protects workers' rights. International human rights groups express concern about worker abuse in the plants. The women who work in the plants, however, have few choices in jobs.

A Korean company employs Salvadoran women to make clothing in this plant in a San Salvador free enterprise zone. These zones make El Salvador an attractive location for foreign manufacturers.

Mining and minerals are of little economic importance to El Salvador. Limestone, gypsum, and salt are the main minerals the country exploits. With no oil of its own, El Salvador imports oil to meet 40 percent of its fuel needs. The country has a small refinery where imported oil is processed into gasoline and other petroleum products. Hydroelectricity—from power stations on the Lempa River—supplies 35 percent. Geothermal sources of energy provide the rest.

Agriculture

Agriculture, including fishing and forestry, provides 10 percent of El Salvador's GDP and employs 17 percent of the workforce. The government instituted land-reform programs after the civil war. However, only 25 percent of landless rural people received land. Wealthy landowners largely retain control of farming. The major cash crops (crops farmers grow to sell, not for their own use) are coffee, sugar, and cotton. Salvadoran farmers also grow flowers for export.

"DOLLARIZATION"

In the modern global economy, countries are increasingly linked together. To make trade easier, the U.S. dollar has partly become the world's currency. Some countries even "dollarize," or adopt the dollar as their national currency. El Salvador dollarized in 2001. This is key to the government's plans to reduce inflation and keep the economy growing.

DANGEROUS SUGAR

Though it is against Salvadoran law, thousands of boys and girls work in El Salvador's sugarcane fields. Much of the work children do on sugar plantations is dangerous. It also interrupts their education. Both planting and cutting cane require children to work in the hot sun all day. Children suffer frequent wounds from the sharp tools they use to harvest cane. Planting cane isn't as risky, but the cane oozes natural chemicals that blister and burn the skin.

The government gives little assistance to the agricultural sector. It believes that investing in the industrial sector will better improve the country's economy. Therefore, the country imports about 30 percent of its food needs.

Migration from rural areas creates a need for farmworkers. Migrant workers come from Nicaragua and Honduras at harvesttime to pick coffee and to cut sugarcane. Both countries are much poorer than El Salvador. The migrant workers earn only about $4 a day, but they get paid in U.S. dollars, which are highly valued.

The majority of El Salvador's rural laborers are campesinos who depend on small rented plots of land to support their families. Subsistence farming is their most important economic activity. They are able to raise barely enough food to sustain human life. Campesinos grow corn, beans, sorghum, and rice. For the most part, their harvests do not enter the cash economy. The farmers may barter or trade in village markets to obtain other essentials. Campesinos' diets often lack nutritional value.

The growing of sugarcane and cacao and the raising of cattle began while El Salvador was still a colony of Spain. Coffee became El Salvador's leading cash crop after its introduction in the middle of the nineteenth century. Coffee is El Salvador's second-largest source of foreign earnings in world trade, after assembly products. The nation is one of the top five coffee producers in the world. It is dependent on world prices for coffee, however. Falling prices have caused a reduction in coffee production.

El Salvador's coffee crop is grown in highland areas. The coffee plants, which are evergreen shrubs about 12 feet (4 m) tall, grow best above an elevation of 3,000 feet (914 m). After about six years, they produce a full crop of small, round fruit, or berries, which change color from green to red as they ripen. After the berries are picked, they are soaked in water to loosen and separate leaves, sticks, and dirt. The two seeds, or beans, are removed from the berries and then washed. Workers spread out the beans on large, flat platforms to dry. After machines remove the thin layers of skin around the beans, trucks carry the beans to a roasting plant. At the plant, workers package the beans for export.

Cotton is cultivated in the southern coastal plains. Fertile soil and an ideal climate make El Salvador's yields of both cotton and coffee per acre among the highest in the world.

Sugarcane production is of two kinds. Large-scale, efficient plantations supply modern sugar mills with cane. The mills process the cane for the export market. Small, inefficient plots turn out cane that is converted into crude, dark, loaf sugar, called *panela*.

The alternating floods and droughts of El Salvador's wet and dry seasons make the lowlands unsuitable for regular planting. Therefore, much of these lands are used for grazing livestock rather than for growing food. Salvadoran farmers raise cattle, pigs, sheep, goats, and horses.

Shrimp is the leading export item for El Salvador's fishing industry. It brings in more than $5 million annually. A new tuna processing plant in the Gulf of Fonseca is increasing tuna exports significantly.

Loggers harvest woods used in dyes. They also cut valuable hardwoods including mahogany, cedar, and walnut. El Salvador is the world's leader in medicinal gum from the balsam tree.

Transportation and Communications

As a small country, El Salvador has one of the best-developed systems of land transport in all of Latin America. Roadways stretch for more than 6,214 miles (10,000 km). About 1,240 miles (2,000 km) of them are paved. The Pan-American Highway links all major Salvadoran cities. Secondary motorways connect the towns of the nation. A four-lane highway links San Salvador with the Pacific Ocean port of Acajutla. Earthquakes and other disasters cause severe damage to roads. Repairing and maintaining the country's roads is an expensive struggle.

More than one half million vehicles use the road system. The number rises every year. Few roads exist within the rugged mountainous areas. There, travelers rely on tough four-wheel-drive vehicles, horses or mules, or their own feet.

El Salvador's roads are dangerous for bicyclists. Signs throughout the country warn car drivers, "Be careful of the cyclist, he could be your brother." (In Spanish: *"Cuidado con el ciclista, podria ser su hermano."*)

El Salvador has seventy-six airports, though only four of them have paved runways. San Salvador's airport, Cuscatlán, is located at La Libertad, about 20 miles (32 km) from the capital. It is a modern facility that serves travelers bound for international destinations. Because of El Salvador's small size and good road system, it has not developed a regular schedule of domestic flights.

The country's railway system has dwindled because of disuse and lack of maintenance. Trains operate on approximately 175 miles (283 km) of track. They are often slow. Passenger accommodations are primitive, but there is rewarding scenery along the routes. The railway connects to the Guatemalan rail system.

Two main ocean ports—Acajutla and Cutuco—serve El Salvador. Boats can travel on only part of the Lempa River.

The government privatized the telecommunications sector in the late 1990s. Close to 1 million land lines and 2 million cellular phones are in use. El Salvador counts four Internet service providers and more than one half million Internet users.

A masked Salvadoran checks a **cell phone** for messages during an August festival in honor of San Salvador's patron saint. In the early 2000s, about one out of every four Salvadorans has a cell phone.

Catch up on the latest news in El Salvador and learn more about its economy. Vist www.vgsbooks.com for links.

Foreign Trade

Political stability has greatly improved El Salvador's foreign trade. The administration of Alfredo Cristiani in the early 1990s had already eased restrictions on imports. The coming of peace brought many foreign investors into the country. These companies benefit from El Salvador's cheap labor, low or no taxes, and incentives offered by the Salvadorans for relocating manufacturing plants.

After the cease-fire, foreign companies made new investments in El Salvador's telephone systems, power plants, and tourism facilities. The manufacture of clothing for export grew rapidly as new textile plants were built. Other leading exports are coffee, sugar, shrimp, chemicals, and footwear. El Salvador imports petroleum, minerals, cereal grains, chemicals, iron and steel, machinery, and transport equipment.

The country's main trading partner is the United States, which accounts for 46 percent of the country's imports. El Salvador imports raw materials for use in its assembly plants. The United States provides a market for 66 percent of El Salvador's exports. The CAFTA agreement of 2006 makes the United States an even more important market for El Salvador. Guatemala, Honduras, and Mexico are El Salvador's other main export partners.

The Future

El Salvador has come far in rebuilding after the violence and destruction of its civil war. The democratic process is strong, and the economy is slow but stable. However, the nation faces serious problems. Much of the population is poor. For many people, life remains a struggle for survival. Discrimination against women remains, and gangs make El Salvador among the most crime-ridden nations in the Americas. Nature continues to threaten the land with earthquakes and hurricanes. Pollution and deforestation further damage the environment. While the government is committed to improving health care and education, many challenges lie ahead. Traditionally hardworking, Salvadorans meet their challenges with hope for the future.

CA. 3000 B.C. People first appear in the area of present-day El Salvador.

2000 B.C. The Olmec civilization flourishes in Middle America.

300 B.C. The Lenca people inhabit El Salvador, based at Usulután.

CA. A.D. 500 Aztecs migrate to El Salvador. El Salvador also becomes one of the centers of the Mayan civilization.

CA. 650 The Aztec civilization falls. Soon afterward, the Toltecs arrive in El Salvador.

CA. 1000 The Pipil people reach El Salvador as the Mayan period ends.

1054 Pipiles establish their capital in the area of present-day San Salvador.

1524 Spaniard Pedro de Alvarado and his troops enter present-day El Salvador.

1552 Bartolomé de las Casas criticizes Spanish brutality in *A Brief Account of the Destruction of the Indians.*

CA. LATE 1700S Cattle, cacao, and indigo production becomes widespread.

1811 Salvadoran José Matías Delgado starts a revolt to gain independence. Spain defeats the rebels.

1821 On September 15, Central America declares independence from Spain.

1823 El Salvador becomes part of the United Provinces of Central America.

1838 The United Provinces collapses. El Salvador becomes an independent republic.

1841 The University of El Salvador becomes the first university in the country.

1870S Coffee becomes so economically important, Salvadorans call it King Coffee.

1882 The government passes a law against communal land ownership. By the late 1800s, about 2 percent of Salvadorans own 75 percent of the land.

1912 The government founds the National Guard.

1932 President Hernández orders the brutal repression of a campesinos' uprising, known as *la matanza,* or the massacre.

1960 El Salvador joins the Central American Common Market (CACM).

1969 The four-day "Soccer War" between El Salvador and Honduras leads to the end of the CACM.

1980 Civil war breaks out. Death squads terrorize civilians. Archbishop Romero is assassinated. Rebel groups form the FMLN (Farabundo Martí National Liberation Front).

1981   In December soldiers kill more than seven hundred civilians in El Mozote.

1984   Newly elected President Duarte counts on U.S. military aid to fight the FMLN.

1986   An earthquake in San Salvador registers 7.5 on the Richter scale.

1992   On January 16, the signing of the Peace Accords ends the civil war.

1994   ARENA leader Armando Calderon Sol wins El Salvador's first postwar presidential election. The FMLN wins seats in the legislature. Salvadoran gang members create a crime wave.

1998   Hurricane Mitch hits El Salvador with winds up to 180 miles (290 km) per hour.

2000   Modern Library names Manlio Argueta's novel *Un dia en la vida (One Day of Life)* as the fifth-best Latin American novel of the twentieth century.

2001   El Salvador adopts the United States dollar. Two earthquakes kill and injure thousands and leave 1.5 million people without shelter.

2002   Health-care workers successfully oppose the government's plan to privatize the national health care system.

2004   Voters elect Elías Antonio "Tony" Saca as president. Ana Vilma de Escobar becomes El Salvador's first woman vice president.

2005   Santa Ana Volcano erupts for the first time since 1904. Tropical Storm Stan causes chaos along the coast.

2006   El Salvador implements the Central America Free Trade Agreement (CAFTA) with the United States. El Salvador and Honduras settle their border dispute.

2007   A $22.2 million project, funded by the UN International Fund for Agricultural Development (IFAD) and the El Salvadoran government, gets underway to help more than seventy thousand subsistence farmers start their own agricultural businesses.

COUNTRY NAME Republic of El Salvador

AREA 8,124 square miles (21,041 square kilometers)

MAIN LANDFORMS Coastal Lowlands, Sierra Madre mountain range, Cental Highlands, Interior Highlands, Santa Ana Volcano (also called Ilamatepec), and Izalco Volcano

HIGHEST POINT Montecristo, 7,933 ft (2,418 m) above sea level

LOWEST POINT Sea level

MAJOR RIVERS La Paz, Lempa, San Miguel

ANIMALS butterflies, hummingbirds, quetzal, toucans, vultures, alligators, boa constrictors, caimans, crocodiles, iguanas, rattlesnakes, anchovies, mullet, shrimp, sea bass, sea turtles, sharks, tuna, armadillos, coyotes, deer, jaguars, margays, ocelots, peccaries, pumas, rabbits, squirrels, tapirs, weasels

CAPITAL CITY San Salvador

OTHER MAJOR CITIES Acajutla, La Unión, Santa Ana, San Miguel, Sonsonate

OFFICIAL LANGUAGE Spanish

MONETARY UNIT U.S. dollar

CURRENCY

El Salvador adopted the U.S. dollar *(right)* on January 1, 2001. The old currency, colones (1 colon = 100 centavos), is no longer used.

El Salvador's flag is composed of three stripes and a coat of arms. The top and bottom stripes are blue. The center stripe is white. Its color stands for peace. The national coat of arms sits in the middle of the white stripe. The coat of arms features a central triangle, representing equality. Five flags circle the triangle, representing the original countries of Central America. El Salvador adopted its flag in 1912.

El Salvador adopted its national anthem—"Saludemos la patria orgullosos" ("We Proudly Salute the Fatherland")—in 1853. Poet Juan José Cañas wrote the words, and Juan Aberle wrote the music. Following is a translation of the first verse of the anthem.

Saludemos la patria orgullosos (We Proudly Salute the Fatherland)
Of peace enjoyed in perfect happiness,
El Salvador has always nobly dreamed.
To achieve this has been its eternal proposition,
To keep it, its greatest glory.
With inviolable faith, it eagerly follows
The way of progress
In order to fulfill its high destiny
And achieve a happy future.
A stern barrier protects it
Against the clash of vile disloyalty,
Ever since the day when its lofty banner,
In letters of blood, wrote "Freedom,"
Wrote "Freedom," wrote "Freedom."

Listen to El Salvador's national anthem. Visit www.vgsbooks.com for a link.

Note: Some Salvadorans' last names follow the Spanish style. The father's last name comes first followed by the mother's last name, sometimes joined with "y" (and). The father's last name is used in the shortened form and for alphabetization. For instance, Romero y Galdámez is known as Romero.

CLARIBEL ALEGRÍA (b. 1924) Alegría is a Salvadoran writer of poetry, novels, nonfiction, and children's tales. She was born in Estelí, Nicaragua, and grew up near Santa Ana, El Salvador. She considers Nicaragua her fatherland and El Salvador her motherland. She went to college in the United States. Alegría's writing reflects the concerns of the Committed Generation group that arose in Central America during the 1950s. Like other writers in the group, Alegría speaks passionately for justice and freedom. Alegría's many books include *Sorrow* (1999), about the death of her husband and translator, Darwin Flakoll. Her writings are available in many languages, and Bill Moyers' PBS television series, *The Language of Life*, featured her work.

MANLIO ARGUETA (b. 1935) Argueta, one of El Salvador's most famous writers, was born in San Miguel. He studied law in San Salvador, where he met other students committed to writing about politics and social justice. His group of writer friends became known as El Salvador's Committed Generation and included Roque Dalton. Argueta has won many awards. In 2000 El Salvador officially declared him the country's most distinguished living writer. His novel *One Day of Life*, once banned by the government, is required reading in Salvadoran public schools.

ANA VILMA DE ESCOBAR (b. 1954) In 2004 Salvadorans elected Escobar to be El Salvador's first female vice president. She and President Saca are members of the ARENA party. De Escobar studied economics in San Salvador and literature in France. During most of the civil war, she worked in Washington, D.C., for USAID (United States Agency for International Development, a U.S. government agency that aids other countries). She managed a $50 million project that promoted economic growth for El Salvador. After 1992 de Escobar worked in El Salvador's banking sector. Under President Flores, she served in the cabinet (group of government advisers). She also served as president of the Salvadoran Institute of Social Security. She and her husband have one daughter.

RAÚL DÍAZ ARCE (b. 1970) Díaz Arce, a Salvadoran soccer player, was born in San Miguel. He was the top scorer for El Salvador's national team during the mid-1990s. He scored thirty-nine goals in fifty-five games. In 1996 Díaz Arce signed with Major League Soccer, the leading soccer league in the United States. He has played for several teams since then. In 2004 Díaz Arce joined the Puerto Rico Islanders and helped the struggling team gain acceptance. He coaches the United States U-17 squad.

FERNANDO LLORT (b. 1949) Born in San Salvador, Llort is an internationally known artist. He works in many styles, but primarily is a painter. His unique art is rooted in folk art—vibrant and colorful. He studied art and architecture at the University of San Salvador. In the 1970s, he founded an art center at La Palma, Chalatenango. The area's mountains and nature inspired his art. He called his workshop there the Seed of God. With his support, artisans of La Palma became well known. Llort dedicates much of his time to encouraging artwork in El Salvador. His art, full of campesino and native symbols, can be seen at the entrance to the Metropolitan Cathedral of San Salvador. He and his wife, Estela Chacon, have three grown children.

VICTOR AND JOHNNY LOPEZ The Lopez brothers are Latin rap artists. Born one year apart in San Salvador, the brothers and their parents fled the country's violent civil war and settled in East Los Angeles. In high school, they returned to El Salvador for two years. When asked in an interview for *LatinRapper.com* about the experience, one of the brothers replied that it was a shock not to have food, indoor toilets, and electricity. He thought that living in the projects was "100 times better than areas in El Salvador." Back in Los Angeles, the brothers formed Crooked Stilo in 1991. Their music combines hip-hop with Afro-Cuban salsa, Colombian cumbia, and other styles.

ÓSCAR ARNULFO ROMERO Y GALDÁMEZ (1917–1980) Romero was born in Ciudad Barrios. He became a Roman Catholic priest and, in 1977, an archbishop. As Romero witnessed government repression, he began to preach for social justice. He was nominated for the Nobel Peace Prize in 1979. His activism won him enemies in the Salvadoran government. In a radio sermon on March 23, 1980, he called upon soldiers to disobey orders: "Any human order to kill must be under the law of God, which says, 'Thou shall not kill.' No soldier is obliged to obey an . . . immoral law." His assassination the next day unleashed an international outcry for human rights reforms. In 1997 the Catholic Church opened a case to declare him a saint, and Pope John Paul II gave him the title of Servant of God. Romero's life is the subject of the American movie *Romero* (1989).

ELÍAS ANTONIO ("TONY") SACA (b. 1965) Born in Usulután, Saca became president of El Salvador thirty-nine years later. He is a descendant of Palestinians who arrived in El Salvador in the early 1900s. His background is in business and sports radio broadcasting. Saca represents a new political generation not rooted in the civil war. He is a member of the conservative ARENA party, but he had little political experience before his election. President Saca supports close ties between his country and the United States.

ALEGRÍA Alegría is one of El Salvador's most scenic towns. Located high in the mountains, it is set among coffee and orange plantations. It has become El Salvador's flower-growing capital. Flowers fill porches, fields, and backyards throughout town. Alegría Lake, a crater lake near town, offers a good place to camp and take hikes in the surrounding mountains.

COSTA DEL SOL (SUN COAST) This 9-mile (15 km) stretch along El Salvador's Pacific coast is one of the country's most popular destinations. A string of hotels and mansions crowd much of the coast, but there are spots to be alone with the warm water, sun, and palm trees. Local fishers launch their boats early or late in the day, and seafood restaurants serve their catches. Surfers take advantage of large waves on the coast.

JOYA DE CERÉN ARCHAEOLOGICAL SITE Ash from a volcanic eruption preserved this pre-Spanish farming community near San Salvador. In 1993 the site became El Salvador's only site on the UNESCO (United Nations Educational, Scientific, and Cultural Organization) World Heritage List.

MONTECRISTO CLOUD FOREST This cloud forest is in the Parque Nacional Montecristo-El Trifinio, north of San Salvador. The rainy area experiences 100 percent humidity and rises 7,900 feet (2,400 m) high. These conditions are perfect for a cloud forest, or woodlands so high they touch the clouds. The forest's leaves form a canopy sunlight cannot pass through. Ferns and orchids are abundant, and mosses carpet the forest floor. Animals include rare spider monkeys, two-fingered anteaters, pumas, and toucans.

RUINS OF TAZUMAL The Mayan ruins of Tazumal are the most important and best preserved in El Salvador. They are in the town of Chalchuapa. In the native Quiché language, Tazumal means "pyramid where the victims were burned." Archaeologists estimate that the first settlements in the area were around 5000 B.C. The excavated Mayan structures date from a period over one thousand years.

SAN SALVADOR The David J. Guzman Museum exhibits items from pre-Spanish and colonial cultures. On display is the important Mayan statue from the 1200s of the god of fertility and sacrifice, Xipe Totex (Our Lord of the Flayed Hide). The Tin Marin Museum for children contains a model volcano that erupts. A civil war memorial wall is in San Salvador's Cuscatlán Park. About 25,000 names of Salvadoran victims of violence are engraved in the black marble wall. The tree-filled park is a good place to rest from the city's smog and noise.

ARENA: The Nationalist Republican Alliance, El Salvador's ruling political party. This right-wing (conservative) party has reformed since the civil war, when it was linked to death squads.

campesino: a poor farmer or rural laborer who usually does not own land

cash crops: crops, such as coffee, farmers grow to be sold rather than used by the farm family

Central America: the narrow bridge of land between North and South America and its seven countries: Belize, Costa Rica, El Salvador, Guatemala, Honduras, Nicaragua, and Panama

colony: a territory ruled and occupied by a foreign power

death squads: pro-government military groups during El Salvador's civil war. Death squads used terror, torture, and murder to control civilians.

FMLN: Farabundo Martí National Liberation Front, founded in 1980 as a union of five rebel armies. Since 1992 the FMLN functions as a left-wing (liberal) political party.

gross domestic product (GDP): the value of goods and services produced in a country in a year

guerrillas: roving bands of rebel fighters. Guerrillas use irregular tactics such as ambushes and hit-and-run strikes. *Guerrilla* means "little war" in Spanish.

left wing: a liberal political position. Leftists usually value social and economic equality over individual freedoms.

literacy: the ability to read and write a basic sentence. A country's literacy rate is one of the indicators of its level of human development.

maquiladora: a factory in a free enterprise zone where Salvadorans assemble goods, mostly clothing, for export

mestizo: a person of mixed European (usually Spanish) and indigenous ancestry. Most Salvadorans are mestizos.

plantations: large farms, or haciendas, producing cash crops such as coffee. Plantations require many workers to operate.

right wing: a conservative political position. Rightists usually value individual freedoms more than social and economic equality.

Glossary

Selected Bibliography

BBC News. 2006.
http://www.bbc.co.uk (October 2006).
The World Edition of the BBC (British Broadcasting Corporation) News is updated throughout the day, every day. The BBC is a source for comprehensive news coverage about El Salvador and also provides a country profile.

Boland, Roy C. *Culture and Customs of El Salvador*. Westport, CT: Greenwood Press, 2001.
This book offers an in-depth look at Salvadoran social life and customs, including religion, literature, and the arts.

***Central America 2005*. Harpers Ferry, WV: Stryker-Post, 2005.**
The article on El Salvador in this annual volume of the World Today series provides a moderately detailed look at the recent culture, politics, and economics of the country.

Central Intelligence Agency (CIA). "El Salvador." *The World Factbook*. 2006.
http://www.cia.gov/cia/publications/factbook/geos/ml.html (May 2006).
This CIA website provides facts and figures on El Salvador's geography, people, government, economy, communications, transportation, military, and more.

"Crooked Stilo: Urban Regional Veteranos." *LatinRapper.com*. April 1, 2005.
http://www.latinrapper.com/featurednews32.html (June 2006).
In this interview, rap musicians Victor and Johnny Lopez discuss their Salvadoran roots. The brothers live in Los Angeles, California, and formed the Latin rap group Crooked Stilo in 1991.

The *Economist*. 2006.
http://www.economist.com (May 2006).
A weekly British magazine available online or in print, the *Economist* provides in-depth coverage of international news, including El Salvador's political and economic news. The *Economist* also offers country profiles with relevant articles as well as some statistics at http://www.economist.com/countries.

Golden, Renny. *The Hour of the Poor, the Hour of Women: Salvadoran Women Speak*. New York: Crossroad, 1991.

This book tells the stories of a wide variety of Salvadoran women during the civil war, often in their own words. The book presents women in Christian movements for social justice and campesino women talking about their lives. It also describes several women killed in the war. An interview with Commander Rebecca Palacios of the FMLN is included.

Jeffrey, Paul. "After 25 Years 'St. Romero of the World' Still Inspires." *National Catholic Reporter*. April 15, 2005.
http://www.natcath.com/NCR_Online/archives2/2005b/041505/041505a.php (June 2006).
This article looks at the life and legacy of Archbishop Romero on the twenty-fifth anniversary of his death. It also covers the recent use of DNA testing to match families torn apart during the civil war. The testing was begun by Father Jon Cortina, a contemporary of Romero.

Murray, Kevin. *El Salvador: Peace on Trial*. Oxford, UK: Oxfam, 1997.
Oxfam is a British international aid organization. Its Country Profiles series looks at international social, economic, and environmental issues. It especially focuses on the everyday lives of ordinary people. This book from the series examines the first few years of El Salvador's transition to peace.

Population Reference Bureau. 2006.
http://www.prb.org (September 2006).
PRB's annual statistics provide in-depth demographics on El Salvador's population, including birth and death rates, infant mortality rates, and other statistics relating to health, environment, education, employment, family planning, and more. Special articles cover environmental and health issues.

South America, Central America and the Caribbean 2006. London, UK: Routledge, 2005.
The long section on El Salvador in this annual publication covers the country's recent history, geography, and culture. It also provides a detailed look at the economy, politics, and government of the nation. Statistics and sources are included too. This is a volume in the Europa Regional Surveys of the World series.

"Turning a Blind Eye: Hazardous Child Labor in El Salvador's Sugarcane Cultivation." *Human Rights Watch*. Vol. 16, No. 2 (B). June 2004.
http://www.hrw.org/reports/2004/elsalvador0604/ (May 2006).
This report is the result of an investigation into the use of child labor in El Salvador's sugar plantations. It includes interviews with child workers about their work and the use of dangerous tools.

U.S. Department of State, Bureau of Western Hemisphere Affairs. *Background Note: El Salvador*. December 2005.
http://www.state.gov/r/pa/ei/bgn/2033.htm (May 2006).
The background notes of the U.S. State Department supply a profile of El Salvador's people, history, government, political conditions, economy, and more.

Weiss, Hank, and Bea Weiss. *On Your Own in El Salvador*. Brooklyn, NY: On Your Own Publications, 2001.
The authors live in San Salvador, and their travel guide is strong on El Salvador's historical and cultural background. They also cover sights to see and offer maps and travel tips.

Alegría, Claribel. *They Won't Take Me Alive.* **Translated by Amanda Hopkinson. London, UK: Women's Press, 1987.**
This is the biography of Eugenia, an FMLN commander, written by one of El Salvador's foremost writers. Based on interviews with Eugenia's family and fellow guerrillas, this book brings the civil war—and Salvadoran women's struggles—vividly to life. Eugenia often stated that she would not let herself be taken prisoner, saying, "They won't take me alive." Government forces killed her in 1981.

Argueta, Manlio. *One Day of Life.* **Translated by Bill Brow. New York: Vintage Press, 1991.**
This simple but intense novel is told from the point of view of Lupe, the grandmother of a peasant family during the civil war. The story unfolds in one day, during which the military interrogates Lupe's granddaughter. First published in Spanish in 1980, the book is a classic of Latin American literature.

Behnke, Alison. *Cooking the Central American Way.* **Minneapolis: Lerner Publications Company, 2002.**
This cookbook presents recipes and an overview of El Salvador and six other countries of Central America. The region provides a wide range of crops and fresh seafood. The countries share many culinary traditions, while offering their own unique dishes. Many of their traditional meals are a blend of Spanish, Caribbean, and Native Central American influences.

Bentítez, Sandra. *The Weight of All Things.* **New York: Hyperion, 2000.**
Based on real events during the Salvadoran civil war, this novel is told from the point of view of nine-year-old Nicolás. His mother takes him to Archbishop Romero's funeral, where she is killed in the shootings. In the following month, Nicolás is trapped between warring soldiers and guerrillas. After seeing a massacre of campesinos, he comes to believe that violence is not the answer to human problems.

Didion, Joan. *Salvador.* **New York: Simon and Schuster, 1983.**
Novelist and essayist Didion went to El Salvador in 1982 during the civil war. Her book captures the terror, chaos, and political repression in the country. She reports, for instance, "Bodies turn up in the brush of vacant lots, in the garbage thrown down ravines in the richest districts, in public rest rooms, in bus stations."

Embassy of the United States in El Salvador.
http://www.usinfo.org.sv
This site has links to current news and U.S. State Department reports about El Salvador.

"Fernando Llort, A Salvadorian Painter"
http://www.lagavia.8m.net/gallery_pinturas.html
This site, in Spanish and English, displays Llort's art in paintings, tile, and wood.

Foley, Erin. *El Salvador* **(2nd edition). New York: Marshall Cavendish, 2005.**
Part of the Cultures of the World series for younger readers, this title explores El Salvador's geography, history, lifestyles, and culture. Color photos, maps, and charts accompany the text.

Further Reading and Websites

Latin American Network Information Center. *El Salvador.*
http://www.lanic.utexas.edu/la/ca/salvador
This site from the University of Texas has extensive links to sites about El Salvador, covering topics from human rights to mountain biking.

Morrison, Marion. *El Salvador.* **New York: Children's Press, 2001.**
A title in the Enchantment of the World series for younger readers, this book covers the geography, history, culture, and economics of El Salvador. It is well illustrated with color photos, maps, and charts.

National Hurricane Center. Tropical Prediction Center.
http://www.nhc.noaa.gov/
El Salvador is part of the "hurricane belt." The hurricane outlook is available on the website of the U.S. National Oceanic and Atmospheric Administration (NOAA).

Rainforest Alliance
http://www.ra.org/locations/el-salvador/index.html
The Rainforest Alliance states that its mission is "to protect ecosystems and the people and wildlife that depend on them...." The Rainforest Alliance is a partner with Salva Natura, the leading environmental organization in El Salvador. Salva Natura's website is: http://www.salvanatura.org/ (in Spanish). Salva Natura manages El Imposible National Park.

"Report: From Madness to Hope: The 12-Year War in El Salvador."
United States Institute for Peace. *Truth Commissions: El Salvador.*
http://www.usip.org/library/tc/doc/reports/el_salvador/tc_es_03151993_toc.html
The UN Commission for Truth in El Salvador prepared this report in 1993. It thoroughly documents human rights violations during El Salvador's civil war. The report covers the murders of Archbishop Romero and many other violent events committed by both sides in the conflict.

Towell, Larry. *El Salvador.* **New York: DoubleTake Books and the Center for Documentary Studies, 1997.**
Photojournalist Towell captured images of everyday life in El Salvador during the civil war. The photographs in this book show that, as he says, he was intrigued by the gentle everyday acts of life during war, such as "a child at the city dump applying red lipstick."

vgsbooks.com
http://www.vgsbooks.com
Visit vgsbooks.com, the homepage of the Visual Geography Series®, which is updated regularly. You can get linked to all sorts of useful online information, including geographical, historical, demographic, cultural, and economic websites. The vgsbooks.com site is a great resource for late-breaking news and statistics.

Captions for photos appearing on cover and chapter openers:

Cover: The Santa Ana Volcano erupted on October 1, 2005. The eruption destroyed about 2,300 acres (932 hectares) of forest and 430 acres (174 hectares) of farmland.

pp. 4–5 On a plantation in Comasagua, a woman picks coffee cherries.

pp. 8–9 La Libertad boasts a broad beach on the Pacific Ocean.

pp. 20–21 The Mayan ruins of Tazumal cover 4 sq. mi. (10 sq km). Some of Tazumal is buried under the present-day town of Chalchuapa. In Quiché, the Mayan language, Tazumal means "pyramid where the victims were burned."

pp. 38–39 Young people in Segundo Montes do their homework outdoors. A mountain village near El Mozote (site of a 1981 massacre), Segundo Montes was founded by returning El Salvadoran refugees after the civil war ended in 1992.

pp. 46–47 In Izalco, young people wear traditional costumes as they dance the story of Spain's conquest of El Salvador for the anniversary of that event.

pp. 58–59 The San Salvador market is crowded with people and merchandise.

Photo Acknowledgments

The images in this book are used with the permission of: © Luis Galdamez/Reuters/CORBIS, pp. 4–5, 46–47; © XNR Productions, pp. 6, 10; © Cory Langley, pp. 8–9, 17, 20–21, 41, 55; © Getty Images, pp. 12, 25, 31, 33, 34, 37, 49, 53, 61, 64; PhotoDisc Royalty Free by Getty Images, p. 15; © SuperStock, Inc./SuperStock, p. 16; © Richard Lord/The Image Works, p. 19; © Archivo Iconografico, S.A./CORBIS, p. 23; Library of Congress, p. 26 (LC-USZ62-105464); © Bettmann/CORBIS, p. 29; © Gilberto Aviles/Reuters/CORBIS, p. 36; © Alyx Kellington/Index Stock Imagery/Jupiterimages, pp. 38–39; © Sean Sprague/Photo Agora, pp. 43, 45; © Alison M. Jones, p. 50; © Alvaro Lopez/CORBIS, p. 54; © Walter and Louiseann Pietrowicz/September 8th Stock, p. 56; © Earl Young/Art Directors, pp. 58–59; © Brie Cohen/Independent Picture Service, p. 68.

Front Cover: © Robert Escobar/epa/CORBIS. Back Cover: NASA.